Hegel's Philosophy of Right

Also available from Continuum:

Descartes and the Metaphysics of Human Nature, by Justin Skirry
Kierkegaard's Analysis of Radical Evil, by David A. Roberts
Nietzsche and the Greeks, by Dale Wilkerson
Rousseau's Theory of Freedom, by Matthew Simpson
Leibniz Reinterpreted: The Harmony of Things, by Lloyd Strickland
Popper's Theory of Science, by Carlos Garcia
Dialectic of Romanticism, by David Roberts and Peter Murphy
Tolerance and the Ethical Life, by Andrew Fiala
Aquinas and the Ship of Theseus, by Christopher M. Brown
Demands of Taste in Kant's Aesthetics, by Brent Kalar
Philosophy of Miracles, by David Corner
Platonism, Music and the Listener's Share, by Christopher Norris
St. Augustine and the Theory of Just War, by John M. Mattox
St. Augustine of Hippo, by R. W. Dyson
Wittgenstein's Religious Point of View, by Tim Labron

Hegel's Philosophy of Right
Subjectivity and Ethical Life

David James

continuum

Continuum

The Tower Building
11 York Road
London
SE1 7NX

80 Maiden Lane
Suite 704
New York
NY 10038

British Library Cataloguing-in-Publication Data
A catalogue record for this book is available from the British Library.

ISBN-10: HB: 0-8264-9605-9
ISBN-13: HB: 978-0-8264-9605-8

Library of Congress Cataloging-in-Publication Data
A catalog record for this book is available from the Library of Congress

Typeset by Fakenham Photosetting Limited, Fakenham, Norfolk NR21 8NN
Printed and bound in Great Britain by Biddles Ltd, King's Lynn, Norfolk

Contents

Acknowledgements

This book is a substantially revised version of part of a DPhil thesis which I was able to undertake with funding from the Arts and Humanities Research Board. The award of a post-doctoral fellowship by the University of Ottawa then allowed me to work on the book itself. I would like to express my gratitude for this generous support. I would also like to thank my doctoral supervisor, Andrew Chitty, together with Douglas Moggach, for their encouragement and helpful comments on my work.

Earlier versions of parts of this book have appeared as 'The Role of Modern Irony in Hegel's *Philosophy of Right*' in *Bulletin of the Hegel Society of Great Britain* 49/50 (2004) and as 'Kant and Hegel on the Right of Rebellion' in *History of Political Thought* 27(2) (2006).

Abbreviations

Writings of Hegel

Werke – *Werke Theorie-Ausgabe*, ed. Eva Moldenhauer and Karl Markus Michel (Frankfurt am Main: Suhrkamp, 1970).

EG – *Enzyklopädie der philosophischen Wissenschaften im Grundrisse* (1830) *Dritter Teil: Die Philosophie des Geistes, Werke* 10.
Hegel's Philosophy of Mind, trans. William Wallace and A. V. Miller (Oxford: Oxford University Press, 1971). Cited by section (§) number.

EL – *Enzyklopädie der philosophischen Wissenshaften im Grundrisse* (1830) *Erster Teil: Die Wissenschaft der Logik, Werke* 8.
The Encyclopaedia Logic, trans. T. F. Geraets, W. A. Suchting and H. S. Harris (Indianapolis: Hackett, 1991). Cited by section (§) number.

NR – *Über die wissenschaftlichen Behandlungsarten des Naturrechts, seine Stelle in der praktischen Philosophie und sein Verhältnis zu den positiven Rechtswissenschaften, Werke* 2.
On the Scientific Ways of Treating Natural Law, on its Place in Practical Philosophy, and its Relation to the Positive Sciences of Right, in *Political Writings*, ed. Laurence Dickey, trans. H. B. Nisbet (Cambridge: Cambridge University Press, 1999). Cited by page number.

PCR – *Die Positivität der christlichen Religion, Werke* 1.
The Positivity of the Christian Religion, in *Early Theological Writings*, trans. T. M. Knox (Philadelphia: University of Pennsylvania Press, 1971). Cited by page number.

PhG – *Phänomenologie des Geistes, Werke* 3.
Phenomenology of Spirit, trans. A. V. Miller (Oxford: Oxford University Press, 1977). Cited by German edition page number and English edition paragraph number.

PK – *Philosophie der Kunst oder Ästhetik nach Hegel. Im Sommer 1826 Mitschrift Friedrich Carl Hermann Victor von Kehler*, ed. Annemarie Gethmann-Siefert and Bernadette Collenberg-Plotnikov in collaboration with Francesca Ianneli and Karsten Berr (Munich: Wilhelm Fink, 2004). Cited by page number.

PR – *Grundlinien der Philosophie des Rechts oder Naturrecht und Staatswissenschaft im Grundrisse, Werke* 7.
Elements of the Philosophy of Right, ed. Allen W. Wood, trans. H. B. Nisbet (Cambridge: Cambridge University Press, 1991). Cited by section (§) number.

VG – *Die Vernunft in der Geschichte*, ed. J. Hoffmeister (Hamburg: Felix Meiner, 1994).
Lectures on the Philosophy of History: Introduction, trans. H. B. Nisbet (Cambridge: Cambridge University Press, 1975). Cited by page number.

VGP – *Vorlesungen über die Geschichte der Philosophie* I–III, *Werke* 18–20.
Lectures on the History of Philosophy, 3 volumes, trans. E. S. Haldane and F. H. Simson (London: Routledge and Kegan Paul, 1955). Cited by volume and page number.

VPK – *Vorlesungen über die Philosophie der Kunst*, ed. Annemarie Gethmann-Siefert (Hamburg: Felix Meiner, 2003). Cited by page number.

VRP 1 – *Die Philosophie des Rechts: Die Mitschriften Wannenmann* (*Heidelberg* 1817–18) *und Homeyer* (*Berlin* 1818–19), ed. Karl-Heinz Ilting (Stuttgart: Klett-Cotta, 1983). Cited by page number.

VRP 2 – *Philosophie des Rechts: Die Vorlesungen von* 1819–20 *in einer Nachschrift*, ed. Dieter Henrich (Frankfurt am Main: Suhrkamp, 1983). Cited by page number.

VRP 3 – *Vorlesungen über Rechtsphilosophie*, volume 3, transcription by H. G. Hotho of the 1822–23 lectures, ed. K. H. Ilting (Stuttgart-Bad Cannstatt: Frommann-Holzboog, 1974). Cited by page number.

VRP 4 – *Vorlesungen über Rechtsphilosophie*, volume 4, transcription by K. G. von Griesheim of the 1824–25 lectures, ed. K. H. Ilting (Stuttgart-Bad Cannstatt: Frommann-Holzboog, 1974). Cited by page number.

WL I – *Wissenschaft der Logik* I, *Werke* 5.
Hegel's Science of Logic, trans. A. V. Miller (New York: Humanity Books, 1999). Cited by page number.

In the case of works in which the text is divided into sections (§), the letter A indicates a remark (*Anmerkung*) which Hegel himself added to the section, while the letter Z indicates an addition (*Zusatz*) deriving from notes made by his students.

Writings of Kant

GS – *Kants Gesammelte Schriften*, ed. Königliche Preußische Akademie der Wissenschaften (Berlin: Reimer/de Gruyter, 1910–).

G – *Grundlegung der Metaphysik der Sitten*, GS IV.
Groundwork of the Metaphysic of Morals, trans. H. J. Paton (London: Routledge, 1991). Cited by GS page number.

KPV – *Kritik der praktischen Vernunft*, GS V.
Critique of Practical Reason, trans. Lewis White Beck (New York: Macmillan, 1993). Cited by GS page number.

KRV – *Kritik der reinen Vernunft*, ed. Jens Timmermann (Hamburg: Felix Meiner, 1998).
Critique of Pure Reason, trans. Norman Kemp Smith (Basingstoke and London: Macmillan, 1929). Cited by first (A) and second (B) edition pagination.

MS – *Die Metaphysik der Sitten*, GS VI.
The Metaphysic of Morals, trans. Mary Gregor (Cambridge: Cambridge University Press, 1996). Cited by GS page number.

R – *Die Religion innerhalb der Grenzen der bloßen Vernunft*, GS VI.
Religion within the Boundaries of Mere Reason and Other Writings, ed. and trans. Allen Wood and George di Giovanni (Cambridge: Cambridge University Press, 1998). Cited by GS page number.

TP – *Über den Gemeinspruch: Das mag in der Theorie richtig sein, taugt aber nicht für die Praxis*, GS VIII.
On the Common Saying: 'This May be True in Theory, but it does not Apply in Practice', in *Kant's Political Writings*, ed. Hans Reiss, trans. H. B. Nisbet (Cambridge: Cambridge University Press, 1970). Cited by page number.

Writings of Fichte

FW – *Fichtes Werke*, ed. I. H. Fichte (Berlin: Walter de Gruyter, 1965).

GNR – *Grundlage des Naturrechts nach Principien der Wissenschaftslehre* 1796, FW III.
Foundations of Natural Right, ed. Frederick Neuhouser, trans. Michael Baur (Cambridge: Cambridge University Press, 2000). Cited by FW page number.

SL – *Das System der Sittenlehre nach Principien der Wissenschaftslehre*, FW IV.
The System of Ethics, ed. and trans. Daniel Breazeale and Günter Zöller (Cambridge: Cambridge University Press, 2005). Cited by FW page number.

W – *Grundlage der gesammten Wissenschaftslehre/Erste & Zweite Einleitung in die Wissenshaftslehre*, FW I.
The Science of Knowledge with the First and Second Introductions, trans. Peter Heath and John Lachs (Cambridge: Cambridge University Press, 1982). Cited by FW page number.

Introduction

> A thinker erects a huge building, a system, a system embracing the whole of existence, world history, etc., and if his personal life is considered, to our amazement the appalling and ludicrous discovery is made that he himself does not personally live in this huge, domed palace but in a shed alongside it, or in a doghouse, or at best in the janitor's quarters. Were he to be reminded of this by one single word, he would be insulted. For he does not fear to be in error if he can only complete the system – with the help of being in error.[1]

The fact that the word 'system' appears in the passage quoted above suggests that the target of Kierkegaard's criticism is Hegel, who describes his *Phenomenology of Spirit* on its title page as the first part of the *System der Wissenschaft*, and claims that the science of the idea or the absolute, that is to say, his own philosophy, is essentially a system (EL §14).[2]

Kierkegaard's main point appears to be that the Hegelian system does not provide the individual with sufficient guidance as to how he ought to lead his life, so that not even the thinker who constructs the system, in so far as his individual existence is concerned, can remain within its confines. Since the systematic thinker is in fact an individual, this shortcoming leads to a contradiction between the system and the needs of the thinker who constructs it, even though his system is meant to resolve all contradictions. This contradiction between the needs of the individual thinker and the system that he constructs constitutes the error under which the system builder must labour in order to complete the system.

We could characterize Kierkegaard's main objection to the Hegelian system in more general terms, however, as the claim that it neglects or suppresses subjectivity. Although this claim invites the question as to what exactly is meant by the term 'subjectivity', my aim is not to determine the extent to which Hegel's conception of subjectivity corresponds to, or differs from, Kierkegaard's conception of it. Instead I intend to show in what follows that Hegel provides us with a coherent and detailed account of subjectivity, which treats the latter both as a concept and as an historical phenomenon. I intend to argue, moreover, that far from neglecting or suppressing subjectivity, Hegel's philosophy of right represents an attempt to integrate subjectivity into the social whole that he terms ethical life (*Sittlichkeit*). We shall see that Hegel offers a theory of subjectivity which seeks to identify both its essential features and its implications for our understanding of the nature of the modern self, including a set of demands that modern individuals, who have become progressively more aware of themselves as subjects in the course of history, might reasonably make in relation to their social world. In this respect, Hegel's account of subjectivity helps to explain why, for him, modern individuals are individuals in the strong sense of the term, that is to say, people who not only distinguish themselves from others on the basis of certain physical traits or psychological features, but who also think of themselves as having separate and particular interests, certain rights and a conscience.[3] Hegel's theory of modern ethical life will be seen, in short, to represent a concerted attempt to identify the kind of social world into which this strong sense of individuality can be successfully integrated.

The claim that Hegel seeks to accommodate subjectivity within his philosophical system is admittedly not a new one. Charles Taylor, for example, speaks of a 'situated' subjectivity in relation to Hegel's philosophical project.[4] Taylor's understanding of this issue shows, however, how easy it is to misunderstand Hegel's idea of a situated subjectivity; for although he describes Hegel's philosophy as part of the modern search for a situated subjectivity, Taylor characterizes this search as one that is motivated by the question of 'how to unite radical autonomy with the fullness of expressive unity with nature'.[5]

As we shall see, this is far from being an adequate description of Hegel's philosophical project because he thinks that autonomy, in Kant's sense of the term, can be realized only when subjectivity is shown to be in unity with the various determinations of right (*Recht*) that make up his theory of modern ethical life.[6] Autonomy cannot, therefore, be thought to precede this unity, whereas Taylor's notion of radical autonomy suggests that autonomy consists in an absolute independence of anything other than oneself. Hegel, by contrast, is critical of such a conception of freedom because he thinks that it reduces the idea of autonomy to a matter of personal idiosyncrasy and ultimately results in the absence of genuine freedom. This is evident from his remarks on Romantic irony, which I shall discuss in due course. Moreover, the various laws and institutions that make up Hegel's theory of modern ethical life are for the most part the products of human thought and activity, so that his attempt to situate subjectivity within his philosophical system and explain the possibility of autonomy cannot be identified with an attempt to show how individuals can experience a sense of unity with the natural world, which is something merely given. Indeed, Hegel, following the modern natural law tradition, makes a firm distinction between laws of nature and laws of freedom,[7] and considers the latter type of law to be higher than the former type of law.

Taylor is nevertheless right to link Hegel's attempt to situate subjectivity with the idea of autonomy; and in this respect I fully agree with the following judgment: 'Hegel never really abandons the Kantian principle of autonomy. His philosophy represents an attempt to extend and deepen this principle, allowing it to penetrate reality even more profoundly than it does in Kant's philosophy, but it never abandons or compromises this principle'.[8] Yet, for the reasons given above, Taylor's account of Hegel's attempt to situate subjectivity equally points to the necessity of determining precisely how Hegel himself understands the principle of autonomy and how he seeks to extend and deepen it. In what follows, I intend to show that both these questions can be answered through gaining a better understanding of what exactly Hegel means by subjectivity and of how he attempts to incorporate the latter within his theory of modern ethical life. This will require paying close attention to the context in which Hegel employs the term 'subjectivity', because this term has a number of different, but interrelated, meanings for him, so that it is difficult to stipulate exactly what he means by subjectivity in abstraction from the particular context in which he is employing this term, as Hegel himself warns us (PR §26A). Hegel also views subjectivity as an historical phenomenon, rather than as something merely given, and we must therefore gain a clearer understanding of the process of historical development in which he thinks subjectivity has an essential role to play. We shall see, in fact, that although subjectivity is what characterizes the type of being that is capable of acting freely and in conformity with ethical norms, it also constitutes a power capable of undermining the authority of such ethical norms. This aspect of subjectivity leads Hegel to say things that make it sound as if he might well want to abolish or suppress it. One example concerns his attitude towards a type of moral theory which has reduced 'the concepts of truth and the laws of ethics ... to mere opinions and subjective convictions, and the most criminal principles – since they, too, are *convictions* – are accorded the same status as those laws' (PR Preface).[9]

The standpoint that Hegel is here attacking can be described as an ethical subjectivism, since it appears to reduce ethical values to a matter of opinion and conviction, which are of an essentially personal nature, and are in this sense merely subjective. Although we shall encounter standpoints (i.e. the Sophists and Romantic irony) which both exemplify certain aspects of subjectivity and appear to involve a rejection of the idea that there are universally valid ethical norms to which we ought to conform, so that the individual alone is held to be the source of all values, we shall also see that Hegel considers a standpoint (i.e. the 'formal' conscience) which appeals to the idea of universally valid ethical norms while appearing to reduce the latter to a matter of personal conviction. In spite of the problem of ethical subjectivism, I intend to show that Hegel must be viewed as someone who attempts to integrate subjectivity into his theory of modern ethical life, as opposed to seeking to abolish or suppress it.

Hegel's theory of modern ethical life can thus be related to the various senses of the German word 'aufheben' that he identifies. To begin with, this word can mean to preserve (*aufbewahren*) or maintain (*erhalten*); yet it can also mean to cause to cease (*aufhören lassen*) or put an end to (*ein Ende machen*) (WL I 114/107). We could say that subjectivity is preserved in the sense that what is preserved (*das Aufgehobene*) at the same time loses its immediacy or one-sidedness, which, in the case of subjectivity, manifests itself as various forms of ethical subjectivism, so that it is only this immediacy or one-sidedness which ceases to exist. Hegel therefore compares the double meaning of the German word *aufheben* favourably with that of the Latin word *tollere* on the grounds that the affirmative determination of the latter signifies only a raising or lifting up, whereas something is *aufgehoben* only in so far as it has entered into unity with its opposite. In what follows, we shall see how subjectivity enters into unity with its opposite, objectivity, in the shape of the various determinations of right that make up Hegel's theory of modern ethical life. I intend to argue, however, that Hegel's *Aufhebung* of subjectivity leads to an unresolved tension in his philosophy of right, one that suggests that the latter has radical implications of which Hegel himself was perhaps only dimly aware.

In order to show that Hegel views subjectivity as a complex phenomenon that stands in an essential, though problematic, relation to the concept of right, and to bring to light the various ways in which he attempts to integrate subjectivity into his theory of modern ethical life, I intend to look at the following set of issues:

1. Hegel's conception of subjectivity, with respect to both its essential nature and its various implications, including the demands, or rights, to which he thinks it gives rise. Since, as mentioned above, Hegel views subjectivity to be an historical phenomenon, rather than something merely given, I intend to address this issue by looking at his account of the emergence of subjectivity and its consequences. In Chapter 1, we shall see

that Hegel associates the emergence of subjectivity with the formation of the type of being that has become conscious of its capacity to stand in a relation of right to others of the same general type as itself, so that subjectivity turns out to be the result of certain formative experiences which must have occurred prior to the existence of the state. In Chapter 2, we shall see how this being becomes ever more conscious of itself as a subject and expresses this consciousness of itself in various demands, which for Hegel all fall under the principle of subjective freedom, and in various philosophical standpoints, including Kant's moral theory, in which the principle of autonomy is developed. This increasing awareness on the part of individuals of their own essential nature (i.e. subjectivity) will also be seen to give rise to weak and strong forms of ethical subjectivism, which Hegel seeks to counter with his theory of modern ethical life, in which he also seeks to accommodate the various rights that he associates with the principle of subjective freedom.

2. Hegel's attempt to integrate the principle of subjective freedom into his theory of modern ethical life while overcoming the problem of ethical subjectivism. This issue will be discussed in Chapters 3 and 4. In both chapters, we shall see that Hegel's theory of civil society is essential to his attempt to meet the various demands that he associates with the principle of subjective freedom. In Chapter 4, a problem will be seen to arise, however, with regard to Hegel's attempt to incorporate Kant's idea of moral autonomy into his theory of modern ethical life. This problem concerns Hegel's need to distinguish his theory of modern ethical life from a conception of the modern state which he criticizes for being incompatible with the idea of moral autonomy; a conception of the state that Hegel thinks is exemplified by Fichte's contract theory of the state. I shall argue that Hegel's solution to this problem is to be found in his account of right as objectified will.

3. The limitations to which Hegel's attempt to integrate both the principle of subjective freedom and the idea of autonomy into his theory of modern ethical life is subject. In Chapter 5 I argue that Hegel's attempt to integrate these two features of the modern world into his theory of ethical life produces a tension within the latter because it implies a right of rebellion on the part of the poor, as becomes evident if we compare the position that can reasonably be attributed to Hegel on this issue to the one that can be attributed to Kant.

Chapter 1: The Emergence of Subjectivity in the State of Nature

Fichte's Deduction of the Concept of Right and its Significance for Hegel's Theory of Universal Self-consciousness

According to Hegel, a period which lacks an abiding set of ethical laws and institutions will lack proper historical narratives. Any theory concerning such a period must therefore be 'an assumption made in the twilit regions of hypothetical reflection', as he himself remarks in relation to the idea of a state of nature in which 'freedom and justice [*Recht*] are – or were – supposedly present in perfect form' (VG 158/131–32).[1] This might be thought to suggest that for Hegel such theories concerning the state of nature will fail to tell us anything substantive about periods for which no genuine historical narratives exist; and we may therefore doubt that the idea of a state of nature will have the same significant role to play in Hegel's political philosophy as it does in the thought of Hobbes and Rousseau. In what follows, I nevertheless intend to argue that Hegel offers a theory of the state of nature which is motivated by a definite question, a question concerning what must be presupposed in order to explain the possibility of a condition of right. Moreover, the answer that Hegel gives to this question is inextricably linked with the emergence of subjectivity, so that his theory of the state of nature can be used to shed light on what he means by subjectivity.

Ludwig Siep has already shown how Hegel's account of the struggle for recognition, as presented in the writings of his Jena period, engages with Hobbes' theory of the state of nature; and he has also attempted to determine the extent to which Hegel's account of the struggle for recognition corresponds to, or departs from, Hobbes' theory of the state of nature.[2] Siep makes the point, however, that while the account of the struggle for recognition given in the 1807 *Phenomenology of Spirit*, which represents the final work of Hegel's Jena period, appears to be similar to Hobbes' theory, a greater distance can in fact be seen to have emerged between Hegel and Hobbes in this work, as compared to the earlier

Jena writings, with respect to the struggle's systematic function.[3] He also points out that although in the course of Hegel's later development the struggle for recognition becomes ever more significant in relation to the elevation of consciousness to the standpoint of spirit, it loses its central role in Hegel's theory of ethical life or objective spirit, as is shown by the fact that the struggle for recognition does not appear in the philosophy of right.[4] I now intend to pursue this last point in connection with the account of the struggle for recognition given in the third part of Hegel's *Encyclopaedia of the Philosophical Sciences*, which was first published in 1817.[5] My aim will be to show precisely why the struggle for recognition must be viewed as highly significant in relation to the elevation of consciousness to the standpoint of spirit, that is, the standpoint of the social subject which Hegel describes in the *Phenomenology of Spirit* as 'the unity of the different independent self-consciousnesses which, in their opposition, enjoy perfect freedom and independence: "I" that is "We" and "We" that is "I"' (PhG 145/177). We shall see that the transition in question is possible because human beings become conscious of themselves as subjects through the struggle for recognition and its immediate result, the master-slave relationship. This will in turn show that subjectivity is the condition of right in the sense that the capacity of human beings to stand in a relation of right to each other stems from their having certain features for which Hegel uses the term 'subjectivity'.

Although Hegel, like Hobbes, characterizes the state of nature as a violent and lawless condition (EG §502A), dominated by 'uncontrolled natural impulses' (VG 117/99), it should be pointed out that he does not offer a state of nature argument which justifies the imposition of certain limitations on natural freedom on the grounds that it would be more rational to accept such limitations on one's natural freedom than to remain in a condition in which the chances of preserving one's own life are less high. Hegel will instead be seen to base his reflections on the state of nature on the idea of the type of being which has the capacity to enter into a condition of right with others of the same general type as itself. Hegel's hypothetical reflections on the state of nature, as found in his *Encyclopaedia* account of the struggle for recognition and the master-slave relationship, will in fact be seen to describe the kind of formative process that must have occurred in the state of nature so as to produce the type of being that is capable of standing in relations of right to others, a being that is both able and willing to limit its natural freedom.

In order to understand what might have motivated Hegel to offer his own hypothetical reflections on the state of nature, and how they relate to his account of subjectivity, we first need to look at a problem that arises in Fichte's deduction of the concept of right in his *Foundations of Natural Right*; a problem which in my view provided the main impetus for Hegel's attempt to describe what might reasonably be inferred to have happened in the state of nature so as to make possible the transition to a condition of right. One reason for claiming that this problem provided the main impetus for Hegel's reflections on the state of nature concerns the fact that Hegel adopts a position very similar to the one that Fichte adopts at the end of his deduction of the concept of right. This becomes evident, I believe, if we relate some of the main features of Fichte's deduction of the concept of right to the section on self-consciousness which immediately follows Hegel's account of the struggle for recognition and the master-slave relationship in the *Encyclopaedia*, that is, the section entitled Universal Self-consciousness, which marks the transition from the stage of consciousness to that of spirit. As we shall see, Fichte's deduction of the concept of right gives rise to the question as to the genesis of the type of being which forms the subject of right; and I shall later argue that Hegel's *Encyclopaedia* account of the struggle for recognition and the master-slave relationship can be understood as an attempt to answer this question. I first need to show, however, that Hegel's theory of universal self-consciousness closely corresponds to the relation of right that we find at the end of Fichte's deduction of the concept of right.

Although Fichte attempts to deduce the concept of right as a condition of self-consciousness, for present purposes we may restrict ourselves to looking at a problem that arises in connection with the part of the deduction in which Fichte seeks to specify the conditions that would explain the possibility of the claim with which he begins the deduction. The claim in question runs as follows: If a rational being is to posit itself as such, then it must ascribe to itself an activity whose ultimate ground lies purely and simply within itself (GNR 17). It is evident from this claim that Fichte identifies rationality with an act whose source lies completely within the being that acts. This self-determining act, whose ground is not external to the agent who acts, also finds expression in Fichte's claim that the character of rationality consists in the fact that that which acts and that which is acted upon are one and the same (GNR 1). As we shall see, in Fichte's deduction of the concept of right the rational being's positing of itself as such turns out to involve an act of self-determination through which the rational being in question determines itself as an individual. In this way, the rational being, as the agent of change, is active, while, as that which is determined through its act of willing, it is passive, so that the requirement that the being which acts and the being which is acted upon be one and the same is met.

Since the rational being which forms the subject of Fichte's deduction of the concept of right is a finite one, its act of self-positing must, however, be understood as an act which underlies the everyday consciousness' own experience of itself as a rational being, with the consciousness in question being a representational one, whose activity is tied to objects and whose willing is tied to representations.[6] In other words, a finite rational being can act only in accordance with its representations of the objects towards which it directs its activity. Since, for Fichte, the ultimate source of these representations is to be found in intuition, the finite rational being's act of self-positing, through which it becomes conscious of its rationality and freedom, must consist in an act which allows it to achieve an intuition of its rationality and its capacity to be self-determining. Its object must therefore be a limited (i.e. finite) one, by which Fichte means an object that is located in space and time, which form the conditions of intuition. A finite rational being must, in short, gain a determinate intuition of itself as a rational being with the capacity to be self-determining so as to become conscious of itself as such a being. The fact that the object of the finite rational being's consciousness must be a limited one in the sense indicated above gives rise to the following problem: How can one consistently think the idea of a self-determining act on the part of the finite rational being, that is, one which has its ground within the latter, together with the idea of an object which stands opposed to the finite rational being and thus appears to limit its activity? Fichte's solution to this problem is to introduce a summons as the object which allows a finite rational being to gain a representation of itself as an essentially rational and self-determining type of being.

Fichte claims that this summons allows us to think of 'the subject's being-determined as *its being-determined to be self-determining*' (GNR 33). His reasons for making this claim are as follows: The summons requires the subject to whom it is addressed to exercise its efficacy, that is to say, to choose from among a whole range of possible actions or even to choose not to act at all; it does not, therefore, require the subject to whom it is addressed to act in any particular way, so that in this respect the summons does not determine this subject but instead allows the latter to be self-determining. The summons presupposes, moreover, the freedom and rationality of the subject to whom it is addressed, since it only makes sense to summon someone to exercise his efficacy if one believes that he has the capacity to act freely and to understand the demand to do so. Consequently, by comprehending the summons in which its freedom and rationality are presupposed, the finite rational being is able to become conscious of itself as a rational being by means of a determinate representation. However, in relation to Hegel's theory of universal self-consciousness, the implications of Fichte's solution to the problem that he is seeking to resolve, rather than the solution itself (i.e. the summons), are of most interest to us. These implications nevertheless require saying something more about the nature of the summons which Fichte introduces in order to solve the problem as to how the finite rational being that forms the subject of his deduction of the concept of right can be thought to remain self-determining when its act of willing is determined by the object of its representational form of consciousness.

From some remarks that he makes concerning the summons, it is evident that Fichte does not think that it needs to be expressed in words; he instead appears to identify the summons with a type of act: the act of limiting one's own activity in relation to others. To begin with, Fichte identifies the summons itself with the exercise of efficacy (GNR 41); and he then goes on to identify this exercise of efficacy with an act of self-limitation (*Selbstbeschränkung*), with the being that summons limiting its own freedom in favour of the formal freedom of the subject to whom the summons is addressed (GNR 43). In other words, the summons consists in a freely made decision not to act without restraint by simply following one's natural impulses, together with some evidence of this decision. Although this evidence can be of a verbal kind, as when, for example, one states one's intention not to lay claim to certain physical objects, it can equally consist in the performance or non-performance of certain acts from which such an intention might reasonably be inferred. Through this act of self-limitation the subject to whom the summons is addressed is made to understand that a sphere has been left open for him within which he can exercise free choice, or choose not to act at all, as the case may be. In Fichte's own words, the subject who summons another subject to exercise his efficacy 'has, in *his* choice, in the sphere of his freedom, taken my free choice into consideration, has purposively and intentionally left a sphere open for me' (GNR 46).

One implication of Fichte's understanding of the summons is that just as it presupposes the freedom and rationality of the being to whom it is addressed, in the sense that it only makes sense to summon someone to exercise his free efficacy if one believes that he has the capacity to act freely and understand the demand to do so, it also bears witness to the freedom and rationality of the being from which it issues. The reason for this is that the summons itself involves an act of free choice, since the being from which the summons issues could have decided not to limit its own activity, and 'the moderation of force by means of concepts' (GNR 45), that is to say, the formation of the end not to limitlessly pursue one's natural desires and inclinations even by means of violence should this prove necessary.[7] The subject who summons another subject to exercise his efficacy thus demonstrates his own rationality and freedom through his evident capacity to set himself ends and act in accordance with them, as opposed to his having the character of a merely natural being determined by the purely mechanical laws of natural necessity.

As it stands, Fichte's theory of the summons appears to give rise to another problem; for it invites the question as to how the subject who summons another subject to exercise his efficacy came to posit himself as a rational being, which, as we have seen, requires that he was himself the recipient of a summons to exercise his efficacy. Fichte's solution to this problem is to claim that we must assume that the relation between finite rational beings is a relation of 'reciprocal interaction through intelligence and freedom' (GNR 44), with each rational being limiting its activity in relation to other rational beings, which it recognizes as being free and rational like itself. This condition of mutual recognition is one in which the subject who limits his own activity and thus summons another subject to exercise his efficacy is also the recipient of a summons to exercise his efficacy because other subjects have limited their own activity in relation to him. Fichte calls this reciprocal interaction through intelligence and freedom the relation of right (GNR 52), so that the latter must be understood as a relation that is made possible by each subject limiting his own activity in relation to others. This brings me to another implication of Fichte's account of the summons; one that is especially relevant to Hegel's reflections on the state of nature and his conception of subjectivity.

According to Fichte, it is only through the relation of right that individuality first becomes possible; for 'I posit myself as an individual in opposition to another particular individual, insofar as I ascribe *to myself* a sphere for my freedom from which I exclude the other, and ascribe a sphere *to the other* from which I exclude myself' (GNR 51). In other words, it is only through being able to exercise free choice and pursue their own personal ends that individuals come to distinguish themselves from others in a way that goes beyond their having different physical features and their exhibiting different psychological characteristics, which both constitute purely natural and merely given forms of determination. Yet the possibility of effectively exercising free choice and pursuing one's own ends ultimately depends on each rational being limiting its own activity in relation to others, thus allowing them a sphere in which to exercise free choice and pursue their own personal ends without interference from others. Whereas in the complete absence of this recognition of the right of others to have a sphere in which to exercise free choice and pursue their own personal ends, each subject could not effectively exercise his efficacy for any longer than the time in which he is able to secure a sphere of activity for himself either by means of force or because no one else has yet laid claim to it. In short, individuality for Fichte depends on the reciprocal interaction of finite rational beings standing in relations of right to each other, since only this type of condition guarantees each subject a private sphere in which to exercise free choice and pursue his own personal ends, thus allowing him to determine himself as an individual.

If we now turn to Hegel's theory of universal self-consciousness, we can see that it closely corresponds to Fichte's idea of a community of finite rational beings standing in relations of right to each other. Hegel claims that this universal form of self-consciousness is one in which each individual self-consciousness has absolute independence, as opposed to its being dominated by others, while by negating its own immediacy, this same individual self-consciousness does not distinguish itself from others but instead recognizes itself in them (EG §436). Since, as we shall see, Hegel identifies immediacy with the purely natural and merely given determinations which serve to distinguish one individual from another in ways that cannot be viewed as the result of these individuals' own activity, we must assume that this negation of immediacy which makes possible one's identity with others rests on the capacity to conceive of oneself in abstraction from all natural and merely given determinations. By negating the natural and merely given determinations that serve to distinguish one human being from another, each individual becomes capable of recognizing others as being of the same general type as himself; so that 'the mutually related self-conscious subjects, by setting aside their unequal particular individuality, have risen to the consciousness of their real universality, of the freedom belonging to all, and hence to the intuition of their specific identity with each other' (EG §436Z).

This invites the question as to how this identity with others can be consistently thought together with the idea that each individual self-consciousness retains an absolute independence in relation to others; for these two features of Hegel's account of universal self-consciousness might be held to be incompatible with each other. The apparent incompatibility between these two essential features of universal self-consciousness can be related to an alleged tension between two aspects of the concept of freedom which Hegel developed during his Jena period that Ludwig Siep identifies: freedom understood as self-overcoming (*Selbstüberwindung*), which involves removing the barriers that separate one from others by renouncing one's particular individuality, and freedom understood as release (*Freigabe*), which demands that one accepts and respects the particularity of both oneself and others.[8] These two aspects of freedom can be seen as reconciled in Hegel's theory of universal self-consciousness, however, if we understand the latter as, in effect, a restatement of the position that Fichte adopts at the end of his deduction of the concept of right, and if we understand the particular individuality mentioned above in two different ways.

Fichte thinks that the subject demonstrates his rationality and freedom, in virtue of which he is identical with others, by limiting his own activity. This shows that the subject in question is not determined by natural impulse alone, which can be explained in purely mechanical terms. The particular individuality that is overcome is therefore to be understood as the individuality of a merely natural being subject to mechanical laws. The act of overcoming one's natural particularity found in the act of limiting one's own activity in relation to others in turn allows these others to exercise their efficacy effectively within the sphere that is thereby left open to them. Each individual thus accepts and respects the particularity of others, while at the same time recognizing them to be of the same general type as himself, by allowing them to determine themselves as specific individuals through the exercise of free choice and the pursuit of their own personal ends. This brings me to Hegel's account of the person, which involves an attempt on his part to define the type of being that is capable of forming part of a single universal self-consciousness.

For Hegel, personality involves both the subject's consciousness of itself as a specific individual and the abstract universality of that which he terms the 'I' = 'I'. Hegel identifies the latter as one meaning of the term 'subjectivity', which in this particular case he describes as follows: '*pure form*, the *absolute unity* of the self-consciousness with itself, in which the self-consciousness, as "I" = "I", is totally inward and *abstractly* dependent upon itself – i.e. the pure *certainty* of itself, as distinct from truth' (PR §25). The self-certainty and absolute unity that Hegel here has in mind can be explained with reference to Fichte's account of the act of self-positing performed by the self in his *Wissenschaftslehre*.

Fichte identifies this act of self-positing, in which the self or 'I' makes itself into its own object, with the concept of the self: for it is only through thinking itself that the self first comes to exist for itself (W 460). It is the way in which the self is identical with the act through which it constitutes itself that leads Fichte to speak of the self positing itself, by which he means that the self's existence is immediately given through the act of thinking itself, so that, '*To posit oneself* and *to be* are, as applied to the self, perfectly identical' (W 98). In other words, the thought of myself and the fact of my existence are inextricably linked because the former implies the latter, even though I may, by contrast, exist without thinking of myself.

The certainty of one's own existence that comes about through the act of thinking oneself is what leads Hegel to speak of the self-certainty of the 'I' = 'I'. The latter's absolute unity thus consists in making oneself into one's own object through the act of thinking oneself, since this is an act in which subject and object are identical, rather than their standing opposed to each other, as is the case with other forms of consciousness. The act of self-positing performed by the self implies, moreover, that the object of which one is conscious is a product of the subject's own activity in the case of self-consciousness, and it thus suggests a link between self-consciousness and the idea of self-determination. In other words, according to Fichte, self-consciousness involves an awareness on the part of the subject of its own unconditioned activity; and this is why Hegel speaks of the 'I' = 'I' as being dependent upon itself.

Hegel claims that 'as *this* person, I am completely determined in all respects ... I am finite, yet totally pure self-reference, and thus know myself in my finitude as *infinite, universal* and *free*' (PR §35). Although the element of pure self-reference can be explained in terms of the absolute unity and self-certainty of the 'I' = 'I', this description of personality also implies the consciousness of oneself as a specific individual distinct from other individuals. In this respect, it relates to another aspect of subjectivity, one that Hegel describes as the arbitrary will (*die Willkür*) and 'the contingent content of whatever ends the will may pursue' (PR §25). Since, as we shall see, Hegel associates the arbitrary will with freedom of choice, this aspect of subjectivity can be seen to correspond to Fichte's view of the person as someone who exclusively makes choices within the sphere left open to him by others, so that this exercise of free choice 'constitutes the person's individual character: through this determination, the person is *the one* that he is, this or that person, called by this or that name' (GNR 56). Hegel therefore views this aspect of subjectivity as being equally essential to the concept of personality as the subjectivity of the pure 'I' = 'I' because it allows each subject to determine himself as a particular person. Hegel's concept of personality thus unifies two distinct aspects of subjectivity within a single concept; and a person must therefore be understood as a type of being whose essential nature is to be defined in terms of these two aspects of subjectivity. As we shall see below, Hegel's *Encyclopaedia* account of the struggle for recognition and the master-slave relationship can be viewed as an attempt to explain how the consciousness of oneself as a person became possible in the state of nature and how this consciousness in turn made possible a condition of right. This brings me back to Fichte's deduction of the concept of right.

Although, as I have argued above, it is possible to understand Hegel's theory of universal self-consciousness as, in effect, a restatement of Fichte's position at the end of his deduction of the concept of right, Fichte's idea of a community of rational beings standing in relations of right to each other presents us with a puzzle: for how did such a community of reciprocally interacting (i.e. recognizing) rational beings ever come about? This puzzle arises because each finite rational being's act of self-positing depends on another rational being summoning it to exercise its efficacy. Consequently, we are confronted with the problem as to how the first member of Fichte's community of reciprocally interacting rational beings was summoned to exercise its efficacy and was thus able to become aware of its freedom and rationality through gaining a determinate representation of this freedom and rationality. In short, we may ask how it was that the first member of this community did not remain a merely natural being, incapable of summoning others to exercise their efficacy through the act of limiting its own activity.

Fichte is led to address this issue when he identifies the summons to engage in free activity not with any single action but with a whole series of actions, which he calls upbringing (GNR 39). This shows that he does not think that rationality and freedom are simply given; in the case of each individual person they are instead the result of a process, which he himself calls upbringing. Yet this reference to upbringing in turn invites the question as to the origin of the kind of community of rational beings in which such a process of upbringing can take place. The process of upbringing which takes place within a community of mutually interacting rational beings standing in relations of right to each other must, in short, be thought to depend on a prior process in which the first members of this community were formed into beings capable of limiting their own activity instead of simply following their natural impulses. Fichte is thus led to reflect on the question as to who brought up the first human couple; and he disposes of this question by citing the wisdom of the Genesis account of the care that God took of Adam and Eve (GNR 39–40). In what follows, I intend to argue that Hegel's *Encyclopaedia* account of the struggle for recognition and the master-slave relationship represents his own attempt to answer the question as to how a community of mutually interacting rational beings (i.e. the universal self-consciousness of spirit) standing in relations of right to each other first became possible.

Hegel's Hypothetical Reflections on the State of Nature

Hegel views the state of nature as a condition in which the family forms the most basic social unit, so that even states of savagery are for him accompanied by social institutions which impose restrictions on freedom (VG 116/98). The restrictions on natural freedom imposed by the institution of the family concern the way in which its members, whose relations to each other are based on feelings of affection and trust, act in accordance with a common purpose shaped by the exigencies of life (e.g. the need to acquire the basic means of survival and to protect its members, especially the younger ones), rather than working for their own selfish interests (VG 118–19/100). Hegel takes this to mean that the members of a society in which the institution of the family represents the dominant form of ethical life do not behave towards each other as individuals or distinct persons with a will of their own (VG 162/134).[9]

Fichte's account of the conditions of individuality in his deduction of the concept of right suggests one possible interpretation of Hegel's claim that the members of a society in which the institution of the family is the most complex form of social organization do not behave towards each other as independent persons. As we have seen, individuality for Fichte demands a sphere in which the subject may exercise his efficacy without interference from others, since only in this way can persons effectively exercise free choice and realize their own personal ends, thus distinguishing themselves from others through their own activity. Yet in a society in which the institution of the family represents the highest stage of development, any attempt to lay claim to one's own personal sphere of activity would be undermined by the need to conform to the common aims and values of the particular family of which one is a member. While beyond the confines of the family, any attempt to lay claim to one's own personal sphere of activity would be rendered highly uncertain and perilous in the absence of the relevant laws and institutions through others simply following their own natural impulses or the desire to gain more control over their immediate environment and other human beings, even if it means using force. Consequently, although becoming a person requires stepping outside the confines of the primitive family, this is not a sufficient condition of personality, since human beings in the state of nature do not necessarily find a sphere granted them by others in which they can determine themselves as individuals. We can therefore identify the decision to limit one's own activity in relation to others as another condition that needs to be met if human beings are to become persons in the state of nature. Fichte suggests, however, that such a decision also depends on the capacity of each finite rational being to recognize others as being of the same general type as itself.

I now intend to argue that Hegel's *Encyclopaedia* account of the struggle for recognition and the master-slave relationship represents an attempt on his part to explain how individuals in the state of nature became aware of their capacity to think of others as being of the same general type as themselves and to limit their own activity in relation to them. Hegel will thus be seen to treat the conditions of individuality found in Fichte's idea of a community of mutually interacting rational beings standing in relations of right to each other as forming part of an historical process, so that history, which for Hegel properly begins only with the state, must be understood as the final part of a more general historical process which consists of three main stages. These three stages can be identified on the basis of the following passage:

> ... the family in itself lies outside that development from which history takes its source. But if this spiritual unit steps beyond the sphere of emotion and natural love and attains a consciousness of personality, we have before us that dark and impenetrable intermediate zone in which neither nature nor spirit is open and transparent, and for which nature and spirit can become open and transparent only through a further process whereby the will, which has now become conscious of itself, develops over a protracted period of time (VG 162/134).

This passage implies the following three stages: the stage at which personality, and hence the understanding of oneself as an individual with one's own distinctive ends and interests, has yet to develop for the reasons that have already been given above in connection with Hegel's views on the primitive family and the kind of society of which it forms the most complex form of social organization; the stage at which the consciousness of personality develops, though not to the extent that it becomes a clear and distinct one; and, finally, the stage at which this clear and distinct consciousness of personality is achieved. I intend to suggest that, for Hegel, the first and second stages belong to the state of nature, whereas the final stage begins with the emergence of the state and its subsequent development in the course of history.

As we already know, Hegel does not think that a sense of one's own independence and an awareness of oneself as an individual, which are both essential features of the consciousness of oneself as a person, are features of societies in which the family represents the most complex form of social organization. I have suggested that the reason for this is that Hegel, like Fichte, holds the view that individuality becomes possible only through human beings reciprocally limiting their own activity in relation to each other, so that each person is granted his own personal sphere in which to exercise free choice and thus determine himself as an individual. We must therefore assume that a process took place in the state of nature whereby individuals not only learnt to limit their activity in relation to others, which is something they would already have learnt to do as family members, but learnt to limit it in relation to others who do not form part of one's own family, and, moreover, in such a way as to become conscious of themselves as individuals with a will of their own. Hegel's attempt to explain this process is, I believe, to be found in his *Encyclopaedia* accounts of the struggle for recognition and the master-slave relationship. In other words, the struggle for recognition and the master-slave relationship can be seen as constituting an attempt on Hegel's part to reconstruct what might reasonably be inferred to have taken place in the state of nature so as to make possible the condition of right which for Hegel finds its most adequate expression in the modern nation state, as described in his own philosophy of right.

As mentioned earlier, in his accounts of the struggle for recognition from his Jena period, Hegel arguably had in mind the kind of natural law theory of the state of nature developed by Hobbes, who views this condition in terms of a life and death struggle on the part of unsociable individuals, even though Hegel does not treat the struggle in question as one concerning self-preservation, as Hobbes does, but instead treats it as a duel concerning honour.[10] The link between the struggle for recognition and the idea of the state of nature as a condition in which unsociable individuals engage in a life and death struggle is also acknowledged in one of the additions to the *Encyclopaedia* account of the struggle for recognition derived from lecture notes made by some of Hegel's students. According to the addition in question, the struggle for recognition in its most extreme form, as described in the *Encyclopaedia*, can occur only in the state of nature in which people are present as isolated individuals (*Einzelne*) (EG §432Z). Given the way in which Hegel associates the state of nature with a condition in which the social institution of the family already represents one form of social organization, we must nevertheless assume that a society in which the family represents the most complex form of social organization forms the implicit background against which the struggle for recognition takes place even in Hegel's *Encyclopaedia* account of it. Moreover, Hegel's claim that individuality has yet to develop in societies in which the institution of the family is the dominant form of ethical life implies that the isolated individuals who confront each other in the struggle for recognition are not individuals in the strong sense of the term. I now intend to interpret Hegel's *Encyclopaedia* account of the struggle for recognition in a way that takes into account the context from which it has been abstracted in order to be treated as a form of consciousness as such.

Hegel's *Encyclopaedia* account of the struggle for recognition closely relates to his theory of self-consciousness. The self-consciousness in question is the self-certain 'I' = 'I', which Hegel identifies as being both an essential aspect of subjectivity and a constitutive feature of personality. Hegel associates the 'I' = 'I' with abstract freedom, which he distinguishes from actual freedom on the grounds that abstract freedom constitutes only the foundation of actual freedom, which also involves knowing that one is free (EG §424, including Z). Hegel's reasons for identifying the self-certainty of the 'I' = 'I' with abstract freedom can be explained with reference to Kant's account of the transcendental unity of apperception.

In the section of his *Critique of Pure Reason* entitled the Transcendental Deduction (KRV A 95–130/B 129–69), Kant seeks to identify the conditions of the possibility of the general experience to which all our particular experiences belong; and amongst these conditions he includes self-consciousness, or the transcendental unity of apperception, as he calls it. According to Kant, a single self-consciousness must be considered to be a condition of experience in general because, in order to be conscious of the representations of which experience is made up, the subject of experience must be capable of ascribing these representations to itself. In other words, the subject of experience must be in a position to think of these representations as being *its* representations; for otherwise the representations in question would have no meaning for it. However, since he is trying to explain the possibility of the general experience to which all our particular experiences belong, and not only the consciousness of particular isolated representations, Kant is led to introduce another requirement that needs to be met in order to explain the unity of experience. This second requirement is that the whole manifold of representations must be grasped as belonging to one single consciousness. The subject of such a general experience must therefore be understood as remaining the same throughout all the particular experiences that form moments of the single organized experience to which they all belong. Consequently, the subject in question cannot be thought of as the mere by-product of the unification of the single representations of which it is conscious, but must instead be thought to make the unity of consciousness itself possible by remaining identical throughout all its particular experiences.

Kant's account of the transcendental unity of apperception as a condition of experience in general thus suggests the existence of the kind of self-identical subject whose possibility Fichte attempts to explain by means of the idea that the self posits itself. Like Kant, Hegel appears to view the 'I' as the ground of unity of a single organized experience, for he claims that 'I grasp every object as a member in the system of what I myself am' (EG §424Z), and that '"I" is pure being-for-itself, in which everything particular is negated and sublated [*aufgehoben*] – consciousness as ultimate, simple, and pure' (EL §24Z1). Moreover, Hegel thinks of the 'I' as having the potential to become conscious of its priority over all the particular determinations which it unifies within itself; and this awareness of its priority over all its particular determinations is another source of self-certainty in addition to the way in which the self's existence is immediately given through its act of thinking itself. This self-certainty in turn allows each 'I' to conceive of itself in abstraction from the various determinations that it unifies within itself and thus understand itself as being distinct from these determinations, so that, as Hegel himself puts it:

> 'I' is pure relation to itself, in which abstraction is made from representation and sensation, from every state as well as from every peculiarity of nature, of talent, of experience, and so on. To this extent, 'I' is the existence of the entirely *abstract* universality, the abstractly *free* (EL §20A).

When Hegel speaks of the 'I' as being abstractly universal he can therefore be seen to have in mind the idea that, in so far as abstraction is made from the particular determinations that serve to distinguish one individual from another individual, each 'I' lacks determinacy. At the same time, as independent of all its various determinations, the 'I' is abstractly free in the sense that it can decide to identify itself with these determinations or reject them, and, until it makes a decision, it remains wholly indeterminate.

The self's capacity to conceive of itself in abstraction from the various determinations that it unifies within itself has a number of important implications for Hegel which will be discussed in the next chapter. For present purposes, we can restrict ourselves to looking at the way in which Hegel's account of self-consciousness relates to the transition from the abstract freedom of the 'I' = 'I' to the actual freedom that is made possible by the struggle for recognition and the master-slave relationship but is fully realized only at the level of spirit.

One important way in which Hegel's account of self-consciousness relates to the transition from abstract freedom to actual freedom concerns the fact that each individual self-consciousness, through its certainty of itself, distinguishes itself from that which remains other than itself. For the transition from abstract freedom to actual freedom is made possible by the move from a form of consciousness in which the self is confronted with an object that is essentially other than itself to a form of consciousness in which it discovers itself in its object, even though this object is not itself. As we already know, this form of consciousness is characteristic of the universal self-consciousness of spirit, in which each 'I' recognizes itself in each and every other 'I' and is in turn recognized by them, while each 'I' equally retains its independence in relation to others through being guaranteed a sphere in which to exercise free choice and thus determine itself as a particular 'I'. Since the struggle for recognition and the master-slave relationship immediately precede Hegel's account of universal self-consciousness, we need to determine the role that they play in the transition from the abstract freedom of individual self-consciousness to the actual freedom found in the universal self-consciousness of spirit.

The struggle for recognition begins with a confrontation between two individual self-consciousnesses, who thus have for each other the character of both an 'I' and an independent object that is immediately present (EG §430). Since Hegel identifies this element of immediacy with each self-consciousness' corporeality (EG §431), the appearance of otherness which each self-consciousness has for the other self-consciousness can be thought to include the natural features that serve to distinguish one human being from another human being in so far as they exist as physical objects (i.e. embodied self-consciousnesses) in the world. Consequently, each self-consciousness first seeks to overcome the otherness of the self-consciousness confronting it by destroying the latter. At the same time, each self-consciousness demonstrates its freedom, that is, its independence from all merely natural and immediately given forms of determination, by proving that it is absolutely indifferent to them through its willingness to risk its own life in this attempt to destroy the other self-consciousness; and the relation between the two independent self-consciousnesses therefore turns into a life or death struggle (EG §431, including Z; §432, including Z).

Hegel's account of beginning of the life or death struggle for recognition thus suggests that this struggle allows each self-consciousness to become conscious of its capacity to act independently of all natural and merely given forms of determination, among which we can include both the bonds that unite the members of the primitive family, which are based on natural affection, and the desire for self-preservation which also serves to limit its members' wills. This in turn means that if we reintroduce the context that is otherwise lacking in the case of the *Encyclopaedia* account of the struggle for recognition, it can be said that each individual self-consciousness, through willingly risking its own life and thus proving its absolute independence, transcends the institution of the family, whose end is self-preservation and whose bonds are purely natural ones. This indifference to one's own natural existence can therefore be seen as part of a formative experience in which human beings, acting on unconscious impulse,[11] become aware of their abstract freedom, that is to say, their capacity to conceive of themselves in abstraction from all natural and merely given forms of determination. This amounts to grasping oneself only as an abstract 'I' = 'I', however, whereas a determinate intuition of one's freedom must be gained if the transition from abstract freedom to actual freedom is to be made.

The need to achieve a determinate intuition of one's freedom means that the attempt to destroy the other self-consciousness must be seen as ultimately self-defeating; for while the struggle for recognition aims at the death of the other self-consciousness, such an outcome would deprive the victor of the determinate intuition of his freedom that is to be gained through the recognition accorded it by the other self-consciousness (EG §432Z). One solution to this problem might be a one-sided form of recognition, in which one self-consciousness is recognized by the other self-consciousness as free because the former has proved its indifference to all merely natural determinations; whereas the desire to preserve its own life has proven to be stronger in the case of the second self-consciousness than its desire to prove its absolute independence, which requires showing that it is indifferent to all the purely natural determinations which taken together constitute that which we call life. For Hegel, the master-slave relationship exemplifies this one-sided form of recognition (EG §433).

Although the struggle for recognition involves a departure from Fichte's deduction of the concept of right because the individuals concerned do not limit their own activity in relation to each other but instead intensify it in a life or death struggle, the master-slave relationship constitutes an attempt on Hegel's part to explain how individuals came to recognize their capacity to limit their own activity in relation to others. Fichte, by contrast, is forced to resort to biblical narrative, and hence to religious authority, in his attempt to explain this capacity in the case of the first members of his community of reciprocally interacting rational beings. According to Hegel, it is the slave who becomes conscious of his capacity to limit his own activity, since he is forced to renounce his own particular will and submit it unconditionally to the master's will. The selfish master, on the other hand, ultimately remains a merely natural being subject to the dictates of his own particular will (i.e. his immediate desires, drives and inclinations), even though he has gained an awareness of his capacity to act independently of all purely natural forms of determination through risking his life in the struggle for recognition (EG §435, including Z).

Hegel thus assumes that the master, who is not subject to any form of authority, will inevitably seek to satisfy his natural impulses simply because he is in the position to indulge his desires and inclinations without restraint by leaving the slave to take care of the means of satisfying them. However, it is questionable whether this reversion to the standpoint of a merely natural being on the part of the master is in fact an inevitable outcome of the master-slave relationship, for the master has previously demonstrated his independence of all natural forms of determination and has therefore become aware of his capacity not to follow his natural impulses alone. Although this suggests that Hegel's hypothetical reflections on the state of nature need to be revised, he is nevertheless able to tell us something about the kind of experiences that human beings might have undergone so as to become aware of their capacity for granting others a sphere in which to exercise free choice, thus allowing these others to determine themselves as individuals. For the type of consciousness attained by the slave can be seen to correspond to the type of consciousness required by a condition of universal self-consciousness, in which each individual self-consciousness has independence and yet does not completely distinguish itself from others but instead recognizes itself in them.

The slave's consciousness is formed by two main experiences: the experience of freely risking his own life and the experience of undergoing the type of discipline involved in having his own will subjected entirely to the will of his master. As we already know, the first experience allows an individual to become conscious of his capacity to conceive of himself in abstraction from all natural and merely given forms of determination, with this consciousness in turn making him aware of his potential to be absolutely independent of them. Although the slave's desire for self-preservation turns out to be stronger than his drive to prove his absolute independence, he is arguably still able to retain this awareness of his capacity to conceive of himself in abstraction from all natural and merely given forms of determination; while with regard to the second experience, the slave is forced to limit his own activity in accordance with the demands of his master; and he thus learns to act in conformity with demands that do not necessarily accord with the promptings of his own particular will. In this way, the slave develops the capacity to transcend his own particularity and to think and act in more universalistic terms. Hegel himself stresses the necessity of such discipline when he calls this part of the slave's experience the beginning of true human freedom, with the trembling of the singularity of the will and the habit of obeying being necessary moments in the formation (*Bildung*) of every human being, so that no one becomes free and rational without having experienced the discipline which breaks the particular individual's self-will (EG §435Z). Although Hegel speaks of this process of discipline as being a necessary moment in the formation of every human being, it need not, however, assume the form of a master-slave relationship once a condition of right has been established, but can instead become a matter of upbringing, as Fichte points out.

Since the slave's various experiences not only allow him to become aware of his capacity to act independently of all natural and merely given forms of determination, but also teach him to limit his own activity, he turns out to have precisely the kind of consciousness required by a member of the universal self-consciousness that Hegel terms spirit. To begin with, the consciousness of his capacity to conceive of himself in abstraction from all natural and merely given forms of determination allows him to regard himself as an abstract 'I', one that is of essentially the same general type as others who possess this capacity. This consciousness of himself as an abstract 'I' also makes him aware of his potential to act independently of all natural and merely given forms of determination, that is, his potential to be self-determining. Finally, the discipline to which the slave is subject makes him aware of his capacity to limit his own activity. In this way, the slave is able to grant others a sphere in which to exercise free choice and thus determine themselves as individuals, while these others, by following his example, may in turn come to limit their own activity, thus allowing him to determine himself as an individual through the exercise of free choice.

The struggle for recognition and the master-slave relationship can therefore be viewed as necessary in the sense that when taken together they represent the kind of formative experience needed to produce the type of consciousness required for the genesis of the social subject which Hegel terms spirit. The struggle for recognition and the master-slave relationship thus constitute Hegel's most important hypothetical reflections on the state of nature because they seek to explain how a condition of right became possible, even if they do not mark the actual transition from the state of nature to the condition of right.[12] Once established, a condition of right renders the struggle for recognition and the master-slave relationship unnecessary, however, since the formation of the type of consciousness in question becomes a matter of upbringing, and this is why they no longer have a role to play in Hegel's philosophy of right.

Hegel's reasons for offering such hypothetical reflections on the state of nature can also be shown in relation to some other remarks that he makes concerning the latter. These remarks on the state of nature concern the age of heroes as described in the original (i.e. Homeric) epic. Hegel describes the condition to which the Homeric heroes belong as one in which the state does not yet exist, so that although these heroes stand under the command of one king (i.e. Agamemnon, leader of the expedition against Troy), their relation to him is not determined by law (VPK 86). The various kings are instead independent beings who have chosen to place themselves under the command of a single leader; and the expedition against Troy must therefore be seen as a collective enterprise in which the individual members involved help each other (VPK 291–92). This view of the state of nature thus suggests a condition in which individuals have already escaped the confines of the family and have transcended the stage of being unsociable individuals to become independent members of a common enterprise, which, since it requires that they cooperate with each other, implies that each member is able to limit his own activity in relation to the other members.

Hegel in this way presents us with the idea of a pre-legal age in which individuals consider themselves to be equals and are willing to cooperate with each other, instead of the idea of a condition in which unsociable individuals engage in a life or death struggle for recognition. In this respect, the age of the Homeric heroes points back to an earlier stage in the state of nature in which individuals became such independent beings willing to limit their activity in relation to others whom they take to be of the same general type as themselves. This in turn invites the question as to how these individuals became independent beings capable of limiting their activity in relation to others; and, as we have seen, this is the question to which Hegel's *Encyclopaedia* account of the struggle for recognition and the master-slave relationship is meant to provide the answer. Hegel's account of the age of the Homeric heroes must therefore be thought to belong to a later stage of the state of nature than the one to which his other hypothetical reflections on the latter belong.

Hegel's account of the age of the Homeric heroes raises a problem, however, since master-slave relationships were equally a feature of this age, and we thus appear to have a condition in which independent individuals recognize each other as equals before the master-slave type of relationship has been overcome. Hegel can here be seen to anticipate the objection that recognition can be attained within a privileged race, caste or class within society as a whole, so that it is possible to think of the universal self-consciousness as being a parochial one.[13] We shall see in fact that for him a truly universal self-consciousness is fully attained only in the modern state. Yet in spite of this problem, which arises when we compare Hegel's various hypothetical reflections on the state of nature, the kind of experiences found in the struggle for recognition and the master-slave relationship would still need to be introduced so as to explain the later stage of the state of nature represented by the age of the Homeric heroes, who already form part of a universal self-consciousness, albeit a deficient one, and thus appear to possess the type of consciousness which the slave develops.

Since the type of consciousness in question involves an awareness of oneself as an abstract 'I' with the potential to be self-determining, it must also be thought to contain the two aspects of subjectivity already mentioned: the self-certainty of the 'I' = 'I' and the arbitrary will, which, as we shall see, Hegel associates with freedom of choice. Subjectivity thus defines the type of being which is capable of standing in relations of right to others of the same general type as itself and of determining itself as individual. Although subjectivity can therefore be seen to stand in an essential relation to the concept of right, it also gives rise to various forms of ethical subjectivism, which appear to undermine the idea of universally valid ethical norms. In the next chapter, I intend to look at the reasons that Hegel gives for the emergence of various forms of ethical subjectivism, while also showing how he deepens the conception of subjectivity that we have encountered in this chapter in his account of the moral standpoint.

Chapter 2: Subjectivity

The Sophists and Socrates

Hegel's remarks on the Sophists and Socrates can be used to illustrate some important aspects of his attempt to develop the implications of the conception of subjectivity described in the previous chapter. A significant difference between the standpoint adopted by the Sophists and the one adopted by Socrates will also serve to illustrate the tension that exists between subjectivity and the idea that there are certain universally valid ethical norms. Moreover, in the case of Socrates we encounter a conception of ethical truth which Hegel will be seen to adopt in his attempt to demonstrate the possibility of reconciling subjectivity with the idea of a set of universally valid ethical norms.

As regards Hegel's attempt to develop the implications of his account of subjectivity in relation to history, he suggests that subjectivity began to assert itself at a relatively late stage in the ancient Greek world, and consequently after a condition of right, in the form of the *polis,* had come into existence, even though, as we saw in the previous chapter, he appears to be committed to the view that the emergence of subjectivity first made possible the existence of a condition of right. The Sophists and Socrates are of particular significance in relation to the way in which subjectivity began to assert itself in the *polis,* for they are said by Hegel to have ushered in the age of 'subjective reflection' and were thus responsible for positing the absolute as subject (VGP I 404/350).

This subjective reflection, which involves adopting a reflective attitude towards both oneself and one's social world, is made possible by the subjectivity of the self-certain 'I' = 'I'. As we have seen, this abstract self-certainty rests on the fact that the subject's existence is immediately given through its act of thinking itself and on the fact that the 'I' cannot be identified with any of the determinate features that it unifies within itself. The 'I' is instead conscious of being that which unifies all such determinate features within itself. It can become conscious of this fact because these determinations are not themselves the source of the unity that they exhibit in relation to each other, but instead presuppose something that unifies them; and Hegel, following Kant and Fichte, identifies this source of unity with the unity of self-consciousness. The necessity of attributing to itself this unifying function allows the self-conscious subject to conceive of itself in abstraction from its various determinations, whether they are merely given (e.g. natural) determinations or ones that are products of its own self-determining activity.

For Hegel, the self-conscious subject's capacity to conceive of itself in abstraction from all its various determinations has certain practical implications. To begin with, it allows the subject to renounce all its determinations taken together as a whole. We have already encountered an example of how this might be possible in the case of the willingness to risk one's own life in a life or death struggle for recognition. Hegel also cites the fact that a human being can, unlike an animal, commit suicide as another example of the capacity to renounce all one's determinations taken together as a whole (PR§5Z, 47A). Given this capacity to renounce all its determinations taken together as a whole, we must assume that the subject has the capacity to renounce single determinations, as when it chooses not to indulge a particular desire or inclination that it just happens to have, and the capacity to resolve upon one course of action rather than another, or even to renounce all ends whatsoever. In short, since the 'I' can conceive of itself in abstraction from its various determinations, it need not think of itself as being completely determined by them. Given its independence of its various determinations, the subject can also be thought to possess the capacity to objectify its determinations in the sense of adopting a reflective stance towards them, thus allowing the subject to decide whether or not it wants to identify itself with them. For instance, I might have certain given desires that I do not think reflect my true nature, and I may, therefore, regard them as accidental features which do not form part of my 'real' self, which is held to be independent of them.

The self-certainty of the 'I' = 'I' thus constitutes the very basis of the practical subject's capacity to resolve on one content of the will rather than another and to identify itself with one thing rather than another. I shall later have more to say about Hegel's account of this capacity and its relation to his theory of modern ethical life. Yet it must already be seen to involve a deepening of the conception of subjectivity described in the previous chapter; for a subject's capacity to determine himself as an individual through the exercise of free choice has become linked to an act of reflection on the part of the abstractly self-certain 'I' = 'I'. In this respect, Hegel can be seen to have established a relation between the two forms of subjectivity that he takes to be unified in the concept of personality.

The emergence of subjective reflection therefore turns out to depend on an increased awareness of one's capacity to distinguish oneself from all the various determinations which make one into the particular person that one is, whereas a strict identity of oneself with these determinations would rule out the possibility of such a reflective relation. The emergence of subjective reflection is of great significance for Hegel because he holds the view that a reflective attitude is a defining feature of philosophical thought, which he describes as a 'thinking-over [*Nachdenken*]' and 'the *reflective* thought that has *thoughts* as such as its *content* and brings them to consciousness' (EL §2A). In other words, philosophical thought reflects upon the thoughts that form the content of less reflective forms of consciousness, as when it critically examines such thoughts so as to find out whether or not the claims made in relation to them are valid ones.

Among the determinations that reflective thought is thus able to make into its object we can include thoughts concerning what is ethically right or wrong that derive from custom and tradition; and we shall now see that Hegel's remarks on the Sophists and Socrates show how the relation of subjectivity to such thoughts becomes problematic. Although both the Sophists and Socrates provide examples of the kind of reflective thought which Hegel associates with the 'thinking-over' of thoughts which less reflective forms of consciousness simply accept as something given, this common feature should not, however, be allowed to obscure a fundamental difference between the Sophists' use of a critical approach to that which others unreflectively accept as being valid and Socrates' use of this same approach. Hegel relates the difference in question to the assertion made by the Sophist Protagoras that man is the measure of all things. Broadly speaking, this assertion expresses the idea that man himself provides the measure by means of which everything is to be judged. Hegel argues, however, that this claim is susceptible to two very different interpretations: either each man in his particularity, as 'this contingent man', is the measure, or else 'self-conscious reason in man, man in his rational nature and his universal substantiality' is the measure (VGP I 430/373–74). I shall now show that the Sophists provide an example of the first interpretation of the claim that man is the measure of all things, whereas Socrates provides an example of the second interpretation of this claim.

According to Hegel, reflective thought in the case of the Sophists turns its negative power against the manifold determinacy of the theoretical and practical realms, that is, the various laws and principles which the unreflective 'natural consciousness' takes to be immediately valid (VGP I 409/355). The negative power of reflective thought here consists in its ability to reveal the contradictory nature of any ordinary understanding of the world, so that the various laws, rules and general propositions, or 'fixed essentialities' as Hegel calls them, that the natural consciousness holds to be unquestionably true and binding on it become confused (VGP I 408/354). Although this negative power was the cause of the general outcry against the Sophists, Hegel views them in a more positive light because they showed that it was no longer sufficient for human beings to obey the law as an external necessity, so that individuals must instead seek to convince themselves, through a process of reflection, of the validity of what they hold to be genuinely binding on them (VGP I 412/357). Hegel claims, therefore, that the Sophists taught human beings to have thoughts concerning what should have authority for them (VGP I 411/357).

In the light of these remarks on the Sophists, it should come as no surprise that Hegel himself demands insight into the rationality of ethical laws and principles. He in fact describes the highest right of the subject as the right 'to recognize nothing that I do not perceive as rational' (PR §132A). Hegel associates this right with the principle of subjective freedom, which he thinks is of great importance in the modern world, in which whatever is to achieve recognition 'no longer achieves it by force, and only to a small extent through habit and custom, but mainly through insight and reasons [*Gründe*]' (PR 316Z).[1] I shall therefore have more to say later about the way in which Hegel seeks to come to terms with this right to rational insight in his theory of modern ethical life.

Hegel's positive assessment of the Sophists, which is based on the idea that their critical stance towards given social norms led individuals to question the legitimacy of these norms and to judge them according to whether they were rational or not, is tempered by an awareness that their type of reasoning must, from an ethical standpoint, be seen as subject to a serious limitation. Hegel describes the form of reasoning of which the Sophists were the masters as reasoning from grounds (*Räsonnement aus Gründen*) (VGP I 420/365). The limitation to which this type of reasoning is subject concerns the fact that it is, according to Hegel, possible to justify anything by means of such reasoning from grounds, since arguments for and against can be given for everything (VGP I 424/368–69). The Sophists themselves demonstrated this fact because eloquence (i.e. rhetoric), which employs reflective thought as a means of convincing others, was one of the main skills that they taught their pupils (VGP I 412/358). Hegel does not think, however, that this use of reflective thought is restricted to the Sophists and their pupils alone; he instead thinks that the type of reasoning in question is also to be found in a modern approach to ethics; and I shall try to explain in more detail what Hegel means when he claims that arguments for and against can be given for everything when

I come to look at this later example of reasoning from grounds, which Hegel associates with the 'formal' conscience. For present purposes, it is enough to give a basic idea of Hegel's reasons for thinking that this type of reasoning has harmful consequences for ethics and to introduce in this way the problematic nature of the relation of subjectivity to the idea that there are certain universally valid ethical norms, a relation which will be seen as integral to Hegel's theory of modern ethical life.

As previously mentioned, subjectivity, understood as the self-certainty of the 'I' = 'I', is what allows individuals to adopt a reflective attitude towards any commonly held thoughts concerning ethical truths and values, thus giving them the opportunity of either endorsing or rejecting these alleged truths and values. This provides an alternative to simply accepting ethical truths and values to be valid on the basis of authority, as when certain laws or institutions are claimed to be good because tradition states that these laws and institutions have been sanctioned by the gods. After having helped to undermine the kind of unquestioning acceptance of authority which was for Hegel typical of the Greeks of that time, the Sophists were unable, however, to demonstrate the possibility of a set of universally valid ethical norms that could both command the same authority as the laws, institutions and customs of Greek ethical life and withstand the negative power of reflective thought.

Hegel suggests that one consequence of the Sophists' failure to do this was that individuals came to think of themselves as the only sources of value, with self-interest alone coming to determine what was held to be the right thing to do. Moreover, by teaching them rhetoric, the Sophists provided individuals with the means that would allow them to pursue their own interests more effectively; for this art enabled individuals to make what is good for them appear good for others as well, with one individual being able to convince others that what he considered to be the right thing to do, in the sense of its being in his own best interests, was also the right thing for them to do in the circumstances. In other words, an individual trained in the art of rhetoric by the Sophists possessed the ability to isolate various aspects of the matter and to develop a plausible argument which favoured those aspects that harmonized with his own private interests. Admittedly, the use of the art of rhetoric may have occasionally coincided with a person's earnest convictions concerning what was best for the people as a whole. Indeed, Hegel himself allows that eloquence can be employed by someone who wants both to assert his authority among the people and to carry out what is best for them (VGP I 412/358); and he cites Pericles as an example of this (VRP 4 379). Yet he clearly thinks that the Sophists' type of reasoning had deeply harmful consequences for ethics, as is evident from his claim that the principles espoused by them base the idea of right (*das, was Recht ist*) on '*subjective ends and opinions*' and thus lead to 'the destruction of public order and the laws of the state' (PR Preface).[2] The Sophists' type of reasoning is here identified as a form of ethical subjectivism which reduces right to a matter of personal opinion, which can here be taken to mean opinions concerning what is in one's own best interests; and it is in this sense that the Sophists take man 'as this contingent man' to be the measure of all things.

Hegel nevertheless thinks that there is a standpoint which is higher than custom and tradition and the one adopted by the Sophists. The possibility of this higher standpoint rests on the capacity of reflective thought to go on to discover universally valid ethical truths after it has undermined the authority of ethical norms based on custom and tradition. According to Hegel, it is with Socrates that this higher standpoint made its first appearance. The reason Socrates is so important to Hegel is that he attempts to discover the true nature of the good within himself, through the use of his own reason, as opposed to finding it in an external authority. This view of Socrates' historical significance finds expression in the following description that Hegel gives of him:

> Socrates established the standpoint of inner reflection, the inner reflection on whether something is true, so that the concepts of God, good, evil, beauty and truth are not in themselves immediately valid, but, in order to be acknowledged, must have first made their way through the inner depths (*das Innere*) of man (VRP 4 301).

Since Socrates insists that the good that he is seeking must be an objective one, that is to say, one that all men ought to recognize, as opposed to its simply happening to be good for this particular individual called Socrates, reflective thought is here understood as possessing the capacity to produce something that is not a product of the individual thinker as a particular individual, but is instead 'that which is essential [*an und für sich*] – objectivity [*das Objektive*] raised above the particularity of interests, inclinations, the power over everything particular' (VGP I 444/387).[3] This idea represents an important development because it suggests that ethical truths and values no longer need to be seen as having their basis in an external authority, such as custom or religion, but can instead be understood as inner determinations of the self. In this way, Socrates provides an example of the way in which 'self-conscious reason in man, man in his rational nature and universal substantiality' might be the measure of all things.

Hegel therefore claims that the type of objectivity which was first acknowledged by Socrates is the essential universality in which the truth is posited through thought (VGP I 443/386), as opposed to its being objective in the sense of confronting the subject as something merely given and hence as an alien power. He also describes it as spiritual universality and the truth which, in more recent terminology, is called the unity of the subjective and objective (VGP I 444/387). As we shall see, in Hegel's theory of modern ethical life this unity assumes the specific form of the unity of the subjective will of the individual and the universal will embodied in the laws and social and political institutions of the state. Yet in order to understand why it assumes this specific form, we need to gain a better understanding of the significance that the concept of the will has for Hegel. The significance of this concept was first recognized in philosophical standpoints that are later than the one adopted by Socrates, however. This brings me to Hegel's account of the moral standpoint, which culminates in Kant's theory of moral autonomy.

The Inwardness of the Moral Standpoint and the Principle of Subjective Freedom

Hegel states that morality in general concerns 'my inner determination, the subjective will' (VRP 2 91). We have already encountered one reason that he has for describing morality in this way: the fact that with the appearance of Socrates the search for objective ethical values becomes associated with a form of inquiry in which attention is turned away from that which is merely given and external to the moral subject and the source of ethical truth and value is sought instead within the moral subject.

In addition to this reflective morality, which we shall encounter again in Kant's moral theory, Hegel discusses other examples of the subjective will in the section of his philosophy of right that deals with the moral standpoint. Broadly speaking, these forms of the subjective will can all be seen to involve reflection on the self-determining character of the will. In other words, whereas the act of determining oneself as an individual through the exercise of free choice is treated more or less as a given fact at the level of abstract right, which precedes the section on morality, the latter involves a succession of forms in which personality becomes its own object (PR §104). The moral subject is thus conscious of itself as a being with the capacity to be self-determining, so that the section on morality not only concerns 'the *self-determination of subjectivity*' (PR §104A), but also the demand that the moral subject should be able to recognize itself in anything that others allege to be an expression of its own subjective will (e.g. its actions and their consequences).

This demand on the part of the moral subject to recognize itself in anything that other people allege to be an expression of its own subjective will already has an important role to play in the opening section of Hegel's account of morality: his account of responsibility. In this section, Hegel claims that the maxim which states that we should disregard the consequences of our actions and the maxim which states that we should judge actions by their consequences alone are equally one-sided (PR §118A). The maxim which states that we should disregard the consequences of our actions looks very much like an allusion to Kant, who claims that when judging the morality of actions 'what is essentially good in the action consists in the mental disposition, let the consequences be what they may' (G 416). This claim shows that with respect to the question of moral value, Kant accords that which is inward far greater significance than that which has an external presence in space and time, so that when it comes to determining whether or not an agent's will is a good one, the perceivable effects of his actions are held to be of little account. As Kant himself puts it, 'when moral value is in question, we are concerned, not with the actions which we see, but with their inner principles, which we cannot see' (G 407). The infinite value that Kant accords intentions, which are essentially inner determinations of the will, thus provides a clear example of the inwardness which Hegel associates with the moral viewpoint.

Although he criticizes the maxim which states that we should disregard the consequences of our actions for its one-sidedness, Hegel acknowledges that once a distinction is made between the consequences of an action, which belong to the external world, and the intention which lies behind the action, which belongs to the moral subject's inner world, an issue arises concerning the extent to which an agent can be held responsible for the consequences of his actions: for it is now possible to think that what the agent has in mind when he acts and what actually happens as a result of his actions need not correspond to each other. Hegel's acceptance of the fact that a distinction can be made between what the agent has in mind when he acts and what actually occurs as a result of his actions is evident from his remarks on the right of knowledge. This right is essentially linked to the way in which the moral subject's capacity to reflect on its own activity gives rise to the demand that it should be able to recognize itself in anything that others allege to be an expression of its own subjective will. In order to illustrate this point, I shall now turn to a case that Hegel himself mentions in which the right of knowledge is clearly not recognized.

An example of the way in which actions may be judged by their consequences alone is to be found in the tragedy of Oedipus because the latter had no reason to believe that it was his father whom he had killed or his mother whom he had married; yet in spite of his ignorance of these facts, Oedipus was held to be guilty of the crimes of parricide and incest respectively. Although Hegel argues that Oedipus cannot reasonably be accused of the crime of parricide, he also points out that the legal codes of antiquity attached less importance to the subjective element which finds expression in the concept of responsibility than is the case in the modern world (PR §117Z). In the latter, with its far more developed notion of selfhood, it is, Hegel claims, 'the right of the will to recognize as its *action* [*Handlung*], and to accept *responsibility* for, only those aspects of its *deed* [*Tat*] which it knew to be presupposed within its end [*in seinem Zwecke*], and which were present in its *purpose* [*in seinem Vorsatze*]' (PR §117). This right, which Hegel calls the right of knowledge, thus rests on the distinction that he makes between a mere deed (*Tat*) and this deed together with the fact that I also willed it, that is, the action (*Handlung*) (VRP 2 93), and on the idea that the individual's willing of the deed presupposes a purpose that the agent seeks to realize. Therefore, unlike the heroic self-consciousness of Oedipus, the right of knowledge involves the ability to treat deed, action, external event, purpose, and knowledge of the circumstances as distinct from each other (PR §118A).

Hegel views the right of knowledge as an example of what he calls the right of the subjective will, which he describes as both the right to have rational insight into what I hold to be good or true and the right of the will to '*recognize* something or *be* something only in so far as that thing is *its own*, and in so far as the will is present to itself in it as subjectivity' (PR §107). The demand for rational insight into what I hold to be good or true and the demand to recognize or be something only in so far as that thing is my own might appear to represent two essentially different demands. There is, however, a connection between them that helps to explain why Hegel views them both as examples of the right of the subjective will; for in both cases the willing or, in the case of the true, the knowing, subject has the right to refuse to identify itself with anything that it must experience as being alien to itself. I shall later show how this relates specifically to the idea of being able to gain insight into the rationality of modern ethical life.

In the case of the right of knowledge, the right of the subjective will expresses itself in the demand that an agent must be able to recognize the consequences of his actions as the product of his own subjective will. The right of knowledge cannot, however, be held to be a feature of the modern world alone, since the importance of an agent's knowledge or lack of it with regard to the imputation of guilt was already an object of reflective thought in the ancient world, as is shown by Aristotle's claim that actions done through ignorance, by which he means an ignorance of particular circumstances, cannot be regarded as voluntary ones.[4] In other words, Aristotle's account of the extent to which an agent can be held responsible for an action presupposes the ability to analyse an action into its component parts, such as the part which constitutes the deed and the part which constitutes the intention, as opposed to simply identifying the action with the deed, as happened in the case of Oedipus,[5] who was unaware of the fact that the person whom he attacked was his father and the person whom he married was his mother. According to Aristotle's account of responsibility, Oedipus could not reasonably be held to be guilty of the crimes of parricide and incest since he was ignorant of the particular circumstances.

Although Aristotle's account of the limits of responsibility already implies the right of knowledge, Hegel gives an account of the purpose and the intention behind an action that in his view indicates a fundamental difference between the ancient and the modern world. I shall now describe what this fundamental difference is, since it helps to explain why Hegel thinks that the particularity of the will, in the shape of an individual's needs, desires, inclinations and opinions, must be accommodated within modern ethical life.

Hegel distinguishes between the purpose (*Vorsatz*) of an action and the intention (*Absicht*) behind it when he claims that the purpose can be reduced to a means, whereas the main intention (*Hauptabsicht*) is what ultimately lies behind the action (VRP 4 311). Hegel here appears to mean that the purpose involves the willing of a certain state of affairs by the agent, who has good reason to believe that this state of affairs will be achieved through the performance of a specific action. Yet one might then ask what led the agent to adopt this purpose in the first place, that is to say, what was the ultimate reason for his acting in the way that he did. The action is therefore assumed to proceed from an end that the agent wants to realize and in relation to which the purpose serves only as the means (PR §121, including Z).

In this way, Hegel's account of responsibility ends up pointing to a final end or intention, which constitutes the main interest that an agent has in performing an action and must therefore be presupposed in order to explain the action. Hegel is thus led to regard such an interest as being a necessary feature of human agency in general. This interest, which motivates a moral agent to act in a particular way, in turn leads Hegel to claim that 'the *particularity* of the agent is contained and implemented in the action'; and this leads him to speak of 'the *right* of the *subject* to find its *satisfaction* in the action' (PR §121). Hegel calls this right 'the right of *subjective freedom*', which he accordingly describes as the 'right of the subject's *particularity* to find satisfaction' (PR §124A).

The right of subjective freedom is, however, only one aspect of the more general principle of subjective freedom: the one concerning the subject's particularity in the shape of 'its needs, inclinations, passions, opinions, fancies, etc.', the satisfaction of which is called welfare or happiness, either in its particular determination (i.e. the welfare or happiness of the individual) or in its universal aspect (i.e. the 'welfare or happiness' of everyone) (PR §123). In addition to the right of subjective freedom, the principle of subjective freedom also involves the demand for insight into what the subject holds to be good or true, that is, the right to recognize nothing that I do not perceive as rational; the right of knowledge, which requires that an agent is able to identify an action and its consequences as being its own; and, finally, the demand to recognize something only in so far as that thing is my own, which can be seen to include both the right of knowledge and, as will become evident in due course, the right to insight into what the subject holds to be good or true.

Consequently, as far as the aim of incorporating the principle of subjective freedom into his theory of modern ethical life is concerned, Hegel can be understood as claiming that the emergence of subjectivity and the deepening which it undergoes in the course of history results in the following set of rights:

1. The right of individuals to be held responsible only for those actions which they intended and those consequences which they could have reasonably foreseen as occurring as a result of their actions (i.e. the right of knowledge).
2. The right to expect that one's particularity is taken into consideration, which rests on the fact that each individual is a being with certain natural and non-natural needs, as well as certain opinions concerning how these needs are to be satisfied. This in turn gives rise to the demand that one's own welfare and happiness, together with the welfare and happiness of all, should be regarded as important and necessary ends (i.e. the right of subjective freedom).
3. The right to identify with the objects of one's concern through having

an incentive or inclination to pursue the ends that one does (i.e. the right of the subjective will).

4. The right to have insight into what one holds to be good or true.

Although Hegel identifies this set of rights in his account of the moral standpoint, we shall see that he thinks that it is only within the context of modern ethical life that these rights can be fully realized. Hegel claims, for example, that the idea of the welfare of all is, as it stands, an empty word, for even if the dead and people who have yet to be born are not included in this idea, the question remains as to how it relates to foreign peoples with whom one has no direct contact. He therefore states that the command to love one's neighbour as oneself, which he interprets as meaning the people with whom one comes into contact or with whom one already stands in some kind of relationship, is more rational; yet even when we limit the idea of the welfare of all in this way, it remains, as he himself puts it, 'empty bombast' (VRP 4 338). As we shall see, the idea of the welfare of all gains concretion in the sphere of modern ethical life which Hegel calls civil society.

This is not to say, however, that the only aim of Hegel's theory of modern ethical life is to satisfy the demands of subjective freedom; for it is also meant to set limits to the ways in which the right of subjective freedom can be exercised. Hegel himself alludes to these two different aims and their relation to each other when he states that welfare is not to be considered good unless it is in conformity with right and right is not to be considered good without welfare (PR §130). This gives rise to the problem of explaining the precise nature of that which limits the subjective will and the latter's relation to it; and the further significance of the moral standpoint for Hegel relates to its attempts to deal with this issue.

Hegel claims that although the good is absolutely essential and the subjective will's worth and dignity depend on its insight and its intention being in conformity with the good, the good itself can only be actualized through the subjective will (PR §131). Leaving aside for the time being the question as to what exactly Hegel himself means by this claim, which is an issue that I intend to address more fully in the next chapter, there is a sense in which Kant can be said to make the same claim; for he thinks that the moral good can be identified with the subjective will of the individual in so far as the latter adopts maxims that accord with the moral principle which he calls the categorical imperative. I therefore now intend to turn to Kant's moral philosophy, which involves certain ideas that Hegel attempts to incorporate into his theory of modern ethical life.

Kantian Morality

Kant's moral philosophy represents a continuation of the reflective morality that begins with Socrates, and it involves a number of developments, among the most significant of which are the importance that Kant assigns to the concept of freedom and his account of the relation between ethics and reason, together with the moral principle which he derives from this relation: the categorical imperative. This moral principle is held by Kant to provide ethics with a determinate content, in the shape of both the principle itself and the various duties that it generates. In what follows, we shall see that although Hegel largely adopts Kant's position on the question as to what would constitute genuine freedom and broadly agrees with the way in which Kant links ethics with reason, he rejects Kant's moral principle on the grounds that it is incapable of generating any determinate duties and cannot serve as the means of judging the morality of actions.

For Kant, the highest principle of morality must be independent of all empirical conditions. This demand has its source in his conception of lawfulness, which demands an *a priori* status of any genuine law, including the moral law. Kant demands an *a priori* status of the supreme principle of morality because he is seeking to provide an 'ultimate norm for correct moral judgment', without which 'morals themselves remain exposed to corruption of all sorts' (G 390). In Kant's view, experience cannot provide such an ultimate norm for correct moral judgment because it can give rise only to general rules, which, in the case of practical reason, counsel what has generally proved to be the best means for attaining a certain end. The moral theory of eudaemonism, which identifies happiness as the determining ground of the will, provides a good example of what Kant has in mind when he rejects the idea that morality can be based on experience.

According to Kant, the general concept of happiness, which he associates with a 'maximum of well-being', cannot provide the necessity which is required of a truly moral principle because all the elements belonging to this concept are empirical ones (G 418). One reason he has for making this claim is that individuals lack any principle by means of which they could decide with complete certainty on what will make them happy; and they must therefore instead find out through experience what things on average contribute most to human well-being (G 418). This implies that experience is capable of providing only a general conception of happiness, which may need to be revised in the light of further experience; for what may seem desirable in one respect (e.g. wealth) may in fact prove to have certain undesirable consequences (e.g. envy). Moreover, the fact that ideas of happiness appear to vary from person to person raises another significant problem: for even if a general concept of happiness were capable of giving rise to what Kant calls counsels of prudence, which state the means that must be employed if one wants to achieve happiness, these rules are valid only under the contingent and subjective condition of whether 'this or that man counts this or that as belonging to his happiness' (G 416). In short, it seems impossible to form a determinate concept of happiness which could not be otherwise than it is.

The lack of necessity that we encounter in relation to the concept of happiness shows that we are dealing with a determination of the will which depends on contingent factors that may or may not apply in individual cases. Since necessity is, for Kant, a defining feature of lawfulness and of reason, which is governed by laws, this element of contingency leads him to treat eudaemonism as an ethical principle which involves heteronomy of the will, by which he means the determination of the rational will by an object that remains external to it; so that it is not the will that gives itself the law, but the object in virtue of its relation to the will (G 441–42). To this external determination of the will Kant opposes autonomy of the will, which I shall shortly discuss in more detail. First, however, I intend to show that Hegel fully agrees with Kant when it comes to the claim that the concept of happiness provides an inadequate basis for ethics.

While for Kant the concept of happiness involves a maximum of well-being, Hegel describes it as a condition in which the subject's various drives are brought into harmony with each other (PR §20). Happiness thus involves a process of reflection, whereby the various drives are estimated and compared with one another, so that thought can already be seen to have some power over the natural force of the drives. In spite of the way in which the natural will, with its particular drives and inclinations, is subordinated to the concept of happiness, which is universal in the sense that it unites the various drives and inclinations of the natural will into an harmonious whole, Hegel claims that the concept of happiness involves a contradiction; for, on the one hand, it has the form of universality, while, on the other hand, the content of happiness is something singular which does not correspond to the form of universality (VRP 4 137).

Hegel appears to have in mind the idea that there is no principle for deciding on what exactly the content of happiness should be. This content therefore comes to depend on an individual's opinions concerning which drive or inclination to satisfy in preference to others. In other words, since one person seeks his happiness in the satisfaction of one drive or inclination in preference to others, while another person seeks it in the satisfaction of a different drive or inclination, the content of happiness is always something 'particular, subjective, and contingent' (VRP 4 138). Moreover, since the content of happiness concerns the satisfaction of the subject's various drives and inclinations, which for Hegel are natural determinations (*Naturbestimmungen*), he claims that the principle of happiness (i.e. eudaemonism) contradicts the higher principle of freedom; so that an individual who acts according to this principle alone finds himself in a 'circle of dependency in general, in a condition which is subject to change, a change which comes from outside' (VRP 4 138).

Hegel's remarks on happiness thus suggest that he, like Kant, holds the view that the idea of basing ethics on an essentially empirical concept, such as the concept of happiness, is incompatible with a genuinely unconditioned form of freedom, in which the rational will is not determined by anything external to it. Hegel himself tends to view this unconditional form of freedom in terms of the idea of a will that is not determined by what is merely given, such as the drives and inclinations of the natural will which determine an individual's activity, even though he has some control over them, in the sense that he can choose to satisfy one drive or inclination at the expense of another. I now intend to show that Hegel thinks that Kant's idea of moral autonomy represents the higher principle of freedom which the principle of happiness contradicts. As we shall see below, the link that Kant establishes between ethics and reason is integral to his theory of moral autonomy.

Kant's attempt to avoid heteronomy of the will features an appeal to the idea of the conformity of actions to universal law as such (G 402). One reason that Kant has for making this move is that the conformity of actions to universal law as such represents a purely formal law of the will, which can therefore be seen as independent of anything empirical. Kant claims that this formal lawfulness finds expression in the categorical imperative, which runs: '*Act only on that maxim through which you can at the same time will that it should become a universal law*' (G 421). In other words, an agent's maxim, that is to say, the subjective principle of action which the moral subject makes into his rule (MS 225), ought to conform to the categorical imperative, which, in virtue of its having the form of lawfulness as such, is valid for all rational beings. The moral subject should, in short, attempt to universalize the maxim expressing the course of action which he proposes to take so as to determine whether or not the maxim in question is one upon which each and every rational being would choose to act.

Since the categorical imperative is valid for all rational beings in virtue of its having the form of lawfulness as such, Kant identifies morality with the faculty of reason; and this in turn allows him to develop the idea that the law to which one is subject is at the same time a product of one's own rational will. In other words, genuine moral commands need not be understood as having their basis in an external authority; they can instead be understood as issuing from the rational will which each and every rational being must be thought to possess. Moreover, since all moral commands stem from one's own rationality, human beings must be thought to possess the capacity to legislate their own laws, unless they are deranged or completely at the mercy of their natural impulses. This notion of self-legislation is based on the thought that the moral subject, by subjecting his maxims to the categorical imperative, enacts universal law through his approval or rejection of them. In other words, since the categorical imperative accords with the moral subject's essential (i.e. rational) nature, any enactment of universal law must be viewed as an act of self-legislation rather than obedience to a law which is merely given in relation to the will. Kant thinks, in short, that the will of a rational being is not only subject to the law, but is subject to it in such a way that it also makes the law which it obeys (G 431).

This leads Kant to argue that we must presuppose that we are free, since in order to be able to legislate the law to which one is subject, one must be able to act independently of all external (i.e. natural and merely contingent) factors. Kant terms this capacity to act independently of all external factors, including sensual impulse, freedom of choice (*Freiheit der Willkür*); this provides only a negative concept of freedom, however, whereas the positive concept of freedom consists in the capacity of pure reason to be of itself practical (MS 213–14), that is to say, the capacity of *Willkür* to adopt maxims in virtue of their conformity to universal law as such, as the categorical imperative demands.[6] The negative concept of freedom, which consists in the capacity to act independently of all external factors, is suggestive of the type of being which for Fichte and Hegel forms the subject of right; a being that is not only capable of limiting its own activity in relation to others, but also determines itself as an individual through the exercise of free choice. This negative concept of freedom does not, however, specify a specific content of the will, or at best identifies this content with an abstract idea such as happiness or the welfare of all, an idea whose particular content is largely a matter of contingency. The positive concept of freedom, by contrast, does specify a determinate content of the will, one that the subject ought to will. This is why both Kant and Hegel consider the positive concept of freedom to be a higher form of freedom than the negative concept of freedom.

Kant's theory of moral autonomy appears to provide an account of how individuals can discover within themselves, through a process of reflection, certain universally valid ethical norms. Hegel acknowledges that in this respect Kantian morality represents an advance to a higher standpoint, with the most significant aspect of this advance being the way in which the concept of duty makes possible the transition to the higher sphere of the unconditioned (PR §135). Kantian morality makes this transition possible because Kant emphasizes that duty involves the pure and unconditioned self-determination of the will (i.e. autonomy), as opposed to the determination of the will by something that remains external to it (i.e. heteronomy of the will). The idea of moral autonomy therefore represents Kant's attempt to determine what is morally good without reference to custom and tradition or religious authority, which, unless they have been shown to accord with the essential nature of the rational will, can be considered to be the ultimate source of moral value only at the price of introducing heteronomy of the will, that is, the determination of the will by an object which remains external to it.

Hegel likewise speaks of a type of freedom in which the will has a content that is not alien to it because this content conforms to what the will itself essentially is, and is therefore completely with itself [*bei sich*] in the sense that it does not stand in a relation of dependence to something other than itself, but instead achieves an intuition of itself in its object, even though the latter stands opposed to it (PR §23). The idea of the will's being completely with itself is suggestive of Kant's theory of moral autonomy as a form of self-legislation, and we shall see that the idea of the will's being with itself in its other, which is integral to Hegel's theory of freedom, finds expression in his account of right as objectified will, with the subjective will being able to gain an intuition of itself in the various determinations (i.e. laws and institutions) of right which form its object. The idea that dependence on anything external to the will has been eliminated does not therefore mean that for Hegel individuals enjoy an absolute freedom. On the contrary, Hegel's version of the principle of autonomy will be seen to represent an attempt to reconcile independence with a necessary relation to something other, though not completely other, than oneself. We have in fact already encountered an example of this type of freedom in Hegel's theory of universal self-consciousness.

The freedom which consists in the will's remaining with itself in its object, through which it gains an intuition of itself, is also present in all the moments of the moral standpoint, since they all express the demand that one should be able to recognize oneself in anything that others claim to be the expression of one's own subjective will. These earlier stages of the moral standpoint do not, however, specify a determinate content that ought to form the object of the subjective will. Yet the fact that Hegel thinks that the idea of moral autonomy can only be fully realized at the level of ethical life shows that he regards the moral standpoint in general, even when it seeks to specify a determinate content, as in the case of Kant's moral philosophy, as being subject to limitations that it is unable to overcome. In spite of the importance that Kant's idea of moral autonomy has for his own theory of freedom, Hegel is in fact highly critical of Kant's moral philosophy, which in his view fails to provide an objective ethics that is compatible with reflective thought, which refuses to blindly accept the commands of an external authority.

One criticism that Hegel makes of Kant's moral philosophy relates to its 'empty formalism', which concerns the fact that 'it is impossible to make the transition to the determination of particular duties from the ... determination of duty as *absence of contradiction*' (PR §135A). This criticism turns on the idea that Kant fails to provide a satisfactory account of how the categorical imperative can be used to decide whether or not a particular maxim is morally acceptable. Hegel attributes this failure to the way in which the categorical imperative is ultimately reducible to the law of non-contradiction, so that the endeavour to find out whether a particular maxim does or does not conflict with the demands of morality involves determining whether or not it would result in a contradiction. Hegel argues, however, that the law of non-contradiction cannot be used to determine the morality of a given maxim in this way, since a tautology and its opposite, such as 'property is property' and 'non-property is non-property', can both be seen to accord with the categorical imperative, because neither of them results in a contradiction when taken in isolation from each other (NR 462–63/125; PhG 317/430).

Hegel also suggests that Kant is led to presuppose a given content and is consequently guilty of the kind of dogmatism which his critical philosophy is meant to avoid, since in order to derive duties from the categorical imperative, he is forced to presuppose the morality of certain things (NR 463/125). For instance, in the case of the maxim of increasing my property by denying that I have in my possession a deposit which was entrusted to me by a person who has recently died and left no record of it, Kant argues that the immorality of such a maxim is shown by the fact that its universalization would result in people no longer making deposits (KPV 27). This argument might be thought to presuppose the legitimacy of private property, however.

It is not my intention to argue here that Hegel is right to make these specific criticisms of the categorical imperative, even though various attempts have been made to defend Kant in relation to this issue.[7] For I believe that Hegel is able to offer an alternative criticism of Kantian morality which also concerns the issue of how the categorical imperative is to be applied to particular maxims; a criticism which shows that Kant's theory of moral judgment gives rise to the problem of ethical subjectivism. The criticism in question relates to Kant's account of conscience and the section on the moral standpoint in Hegel's philosophy of right in which Hegel seeks to show how the internal development of the moral standpoint results in the subordination of the universal will, as expressed in the concept of duty, to the subjective will of the individual. This development clearly represents a subversion of the basic aims of Kant's moral theory; yet it can also be traced back to the role that conscience plays in Kant's theory of moral judgment. Hegel's account of conscience thus brings to light the tension between subjectivity and the idea that there are universally valid ethical norms. Kant's account of conscience explains, moreover, why Hegel accuses the standpoint that reduces ethics to a matter of personal conviction of reducing the responsibility for crime and evil to a minimum when it admits the possibility of error (PR §140A).

Conscience

Hegel describes conscience as 'the absolute entitlement of subjective self-consciousness to know *in itself* and *from itself* what right and duty are' (PR §137A). In other words, conscience affirms the right of the subjective will to recognize nothing as good or true that it does not perceive as rational. Hegel makes a distinction, however, between the true conscience, for which an objective system of ethical principles exists, and the formal conscience, which lacks such an objective system of ethical principles. In the case of the formal conscience, since it lacks an objective content, all that is left is the abstract self-certainty of the 'I', which, according to Hegel, is merely 'the certainty of *this* subject' (PR §137). As we shall see, Hegel makes this claim because he thinks that appeals to conscience tend to reduce the idea of duty to a matter of personal conviction.

Hegel admits that such personal convictions can be supported by reasons because each action is a complex event, with various circumstances having together led to its occurrence and with various consequences following from it, so that the formal conscience can analyse an action and isolate various aspects of it, as the Sophists were able to do, and put forward a single aspect as the main reason for its action. The formal conscience will then call this isolated aspect its intention and claim that the latter represents a duty. In other words, whereas in the ancient world a tyrant trained in rhetoric by the Sophists might justify a crime such as murder by arguing that it was necessary in order to save the state from danger, thus appealing to other men's sense of self-interest, the formal conscience appeals to the notion of moral duty, which is alleged to represent something higher than self-interest, in order to justify its actions. An appeal to duty was not made by the Sophists, who for Hegel failed to develop an objective ethics which might have replaced the customs and laws of Greek ethical life that their critical and unethical form of reasoning had helped to undermine, or, as Hegel himself puts it, they did not presuppose the idea of the good as such (VRP 4 379). The formal conscience, by contrast, appeals to the notion of duty and thus to the idea of a good which all men ought to recognize. We may therefore describe the formal conscience as a weak form of ethical subjectivism rather than a strong one, which denies the existence of universally valid ethical truths and values altogether.

Hegel gives various examples of the 'the end justifies the means' type of reasoning which the formal conscience employs to justify its actions, ranging from theft committed in order to benefit the poor to murder committed with the intention of 'eliminating this wicked individual who is wickedness personified, and thereby contributing at least something towards the end of eradicating the bad' (PR §140A). Hegel therefore argues that as long as we remain at the standpoint of the formal conscience it is impossible to determine whether an action is a good or a criminal one, since even 'the *lowest degree* of understanding is enough to discover ... a positive aspect in every action and hence a good reason and intention underlying it' (PR §140A). He then goes on to claim that subjective opinion explicitly becomes the criterion of right and duty when the ethical nature of an action is taken to be determined by the conviction which holds something to be right (PR §140A). Ethics is, in short, reduced to a matter of personal conviction.

I now intend to show that Hegel's remarks on the formal conscience, which can be regarded as a weak form of ethical subjectivism, relate to certain features of Kant's account of how the categorical imperative is to be applied in particular cases, and especially the role that he assigns to conscience. As we shall see, even though the categorical imperative is held by Kant to be an objectively valid moral principle, he appears to reduce particular moral judgments to a matter of personal conviction in his account of how this principle is to be applied by the moral subject. We shall see, moreover, that it is Fichte, rather than Kant himself, who appears to develop the implications of Kant's account of the role played by conscience in the application of the moral law. By tracing the reduction of ethics to a matter of personal conviction back to Kant's account of conscience in this way, I hope to show that Hegel could have made a criticism of Kantian morality which is independent of his other criticisms of it, even though he does not explicitly direct this criticism at Kant.

For Kant's conscience is an 'unavoidable fact', which he describes as 'practical reason holding the human being's duty before him for his acquittal or condemnation in every case that comes under a law' (MS 400) and as the consciousness of 'an *internal court* in man' (MS 438). Kant thus identifies conscience with the way in which each individual must decide for himself which of his maxims do or do not accord with the categorical imperative; and it is essential that the moral subject should be the one to decide this: for otherwise the individual concerned would be subject to an external authority, and this would rule out the possibility of his acting autonomously.

This conception of conscience provides the background to a claim which is, I believe, vulnerable to one of the main criticisms that Hegel makes of the formal conscience. The claim in question is that a conscience which errs is an absurdity. Kant makes this claim for the following reason:

> For while I can indeed be mistaken at times in my objective judgment as to whether something is a duty or not, I cannot be mistaken in my subjective judgment as to whether I have submitted it to my practical reason (here in its rule as judge) for such a judgment; for if I could be mistaken in that, I would have made no practical judgment at all, and in that case there would be neither truth nor error (MS 401).

We have seen that, for Kant, it is particular maxims that must be submitted to the judgment of practical reason, for which the categorical imperative provides the criterion of moral value. The idea behind this claim therefore appears to be that while I can be mistaken in judging a maxim to be a duty (the objective judgment), I cannot be mistaken in thinking that I have submitted the maxim in question to the judgment of practical reason so as to determine whether or not it is a duty (the subjective judgment). In other words, an individual can be mistaken with respect to the judgment which results from his application of the categorical imperative to a given maxim; he cannot, however, be mistaken with respect to the judgment as to whether or not he has applied the categorical imperative to the maxim in question: for having made the first judgment, which is of the kind *x* is (or is not) a duty, it would make no sense for the individual concerned to then doubt that he had submitted *x* to the judgment of pure practical reason. He may, of course, doubt that he has applied the categorical imperative correctly; and it would then be incumbent on him to apply it again to the maxim upon which he intends to act, until he is fully satisfied that this maxim is in conformity with the moral law.

This implies that all that can be reasonably demanded of someone is that he acts in accordance with his conscience by earnestly seeking to determine whether or not the maxims which he submits to the judgment of pure practical reason are in conformity with the moral law; and Kant himself concedes that once a definitive judgment on this matter has been reached 'as far as guilt or innocence is concerned nothing more can be required of him' (MS 401). To demand instead that conscience itself should be subjected to some kind of test, so as to determine whether or not it has judged correctly, would require the decision of another conscience, which passes judgment on the first conscience; yet this would lead to an infinite regress. Kant adds, however, that it is incumbent on an individual to develop his ability to judge whether or not something is a duty, and I shall shortly return to this point.

It is evident from Hegel's remarks on the formal conscience that he regards this type of argument as posing a threat to ethics, and he has good grounds for thinking this. For if one person, who does not doubt that he has correctly applied the categorical imperative, judges that what another person takes to be a duty is not one and may, in fact, even be a crime, even though this other person is equally certain that he has applied the categorical imperative correctly, there appears to be no means of deciding who is right, since in both cases the ultimate source of justification is the same, one's own conscience. In other words, to pursue Kant's legal metaphor, there is no external court to pass verdict on the conflicting verdicts of these two 'internal courts', which possess equal authority in relation to each other, since each individual appeals to the judgment made by his own conscience, beyond which there is no higher authority. It is therefore conceivable that two individuals could arrive at opposed moral judgments through their earnest endeavours to apply the categorical imperative to the very same maxim.

We can see from this that even if Kant's theory of moral judgment were able to explain how determinate moral duties might be generated or assessed by means of the categorical imperative, the generation or assessment of these duties would nevertheless depend on an individual's conviction that he has correctly applied the categorical imperative; and, as Kant himself admits, this introduces the possibility of error. Moreover, since Kant denies that there can be any higher authority which could decide whether or not the categorical imperative has been applied correctly, the fact that an individual's convictions concerning duty are tied up with the application of a moral principle appears to make little difference in the end: for the individual concerned will sincerely believe that what he wills is in conformity with the moral law and therefore a duty, even if others should accuse him of lacking moral judgment. Another criticism of the categorical imperative, in addition to the ones that are usually associated with Hegel, might therefore be characterized as the claim that Kant's account of how the categorical imperative is to be applied leads to ethical subjectivism because it involves the internal application of a rule and thus fails to provide an external criterion which could be used to decide whether or not the rule has been applied correctly in particular cases. I now intend to show how Fichte develops the implications of Kant's position. Like Kant, Fichte holds the moral law to be valid independently of whatever an individual earnestly judges to be a duty; and he therefore claims in *The System of Ethics* that there must be 'an absolute criterion for the correctness of our conviction concerning duty' (SL 165). This absolute criterion turns out to be, however, on a par with the conviction of which it is meant to serve as the criterion.

Fichte's account of the absolute criterion for the correctness of our conviction concerning duty includes the idea that the moral law demands a determinate content which it then authorizes. Fichte claims that the moral law cannot by itself produce a determinate conviction concerning duty, however, because the content of the moral law must in particular cases be found and determined by means of the power of reflecting judgment, which forms part of theoretical reason (SL 165). In line with this conception of the moral law and its relation to determinate moral judgments, Fichte states that 'the moral law is purely formal and must receive its content from elsewhere; but *that* something is its content: the ground for this can lie only in the moral law itself' (SL 166). While the first part of this claim anticipates what is usually taken to be Hegel's main criticism of the categorical imperative, the second part gives rise to the problem as to how the moral law is able to confirm or deny a theoretical judgment. This problem again concerns the issue as to how the moral law is to be applied to a particular content; and Fichte's attempt to deal with this issue involves an appeal to a feeling of truth and certainty, just as Kant's account of the application of the categorical imperative rests on the conviction that one has correctly applied this moral principle to a particular maxim.

In order to explain this feeling of truth and certainty, Fichte puts forward the idea that the moral drive (*der sittliche Trieb*) expresses itself as the drive towards a determinate cognition (SL 166). All this means is that, as mentioned above, the moral law demands a determinate content which it itself cannot provide, with this leading the moral drive to impel the power of reflecting judgment to seek this content. As long as the power of reflecting judgment is still seeking this content, the free power of imagination continues to hover between opposed determinations; and, since the moral drive remains unsatisfied, feelings of doubt and concern arise, because the matter in question is of the utmost importance (SL 167).

Although Fichte does not explain what he means by the free power of imagination in the relevant section of *The System of Ethics*, the idea appears to be that the individual who is seeking to make a determinate moral judgment is initially presented with two or more opposed judgments, such as the judgment that it is morally permissible and even a duty to rob the rich in order to benefit the poor and the judgment that it would be immoral to act in this way. Since the individual concerned does not at first find one of these judgments more compelling than the other, he passes from one to the other and back again until he feels himself forced to adopt one of them at the expense of the other. For Fichte, this happens when the power of reflecting judgment finally discovers that which is demanded by the moral drive, namely, a determinate content for the moral law. This discovery is revealed through a feeling of harmony, which derives from the way in which the power of imagination is 'bound and compelled' because 'I cannot view this matter in any way other than in the way I do view it' (SL 167). According to Fichte, this feeling of harmony and constraint results in an immediate certainty accompanied by a sense of calm and satisfaction (SL 168).

It is questionable, however, whether Fichte's appeal to a feeling of immediate certainty avoids the basic problem which Hegel identifies with the standpoint of the formal conscience, which concerns the way in which the latter reduces ethics to a matter of personal conviction. For however earnest an individual's convictions concerning duty may be, there is always the possibility that others will not experience the same feeling of conviction and may even, with regard to the very same content, feel convinced that its opposite is a duty. Indeed, in the case of Fichte's account of conscience, it appears relatively easy to think of cases in which one individual experiences an immediate certainty accompanied by a sense of calm and satisfaction in relation to what he takes to be a duty, while another individual does not claim to experience the same immediate certainty and sense of calm and satisfaction even though he is faced with the same content, such as the proposition that it is morally permissible to steal from the rich to benefit the poor or the proposition that it is morally permissible to murder a wicked person in order to contribute towards eradicating evil from the world. The second individual may in fact experience an immediate certainty accompanied by a sense of calm and satisfaction in relation to a content that stands in direct opposition to the content concerning which the first individual experiences an immediate certainty, such as the idea that it is morally impermissible to steal or to murder someone regardless of the particular circumstances.

Fichte seems to think that the immediate certainty concerning duty is so distinctive and infallible that it could never serve to justify two directly opposed judgments, and he therefore claims that conscience never errs and cannot err (SL 174). We have seen that Kant makes a similar claim, though he allows for the possibility of error because even if I cannot be mistaken in thinking that I have applied the categorical imperative, I can be mistaken in thinking that I have applied it correctly. In spite of his claim that conscience never errs and cannot err, Fichte may appear to allow for the possibility of error when he claims that it is possible for someone to darken his clear consciousness of what duty demands because this consciousness disappears if one ceases to reflect on it (SL 192). This darkening of the clear consciousness of duty is thus attributable to an inattentiveness or thoughtlessness on the part of the moral subject (SL 193). Yet even if we accept that such a darkening of the consciousness of duty is possible, the fact remains that the clear consciousness of duty consists in an immediate certainty; and this means that an individual who is personally convinced that the judgment which he makes constitutes a duty cannot be said to err, since this conviction is by itself proof that in his own case a darkening of the clear consciousness of duty has not occurred. We may therefore ask what guarantee there is, apart from Fichte's assertion that this moral certainty is infallible, that an individual's clear consciousness of duty cannot err in its identification of particular duties. Indeed, we are now far removed from Kant's ultimate norm for correct moral judgment and very close to an ethics based on personal conviction alone; and, since Fichte simply develops the implications of Kant's theory of moral judgment, it appears that the idea of an ethics based on personal conviction alone merely makes explicit the ethical subjectivism to be found in Kant's moral philosophy.

The way in which the idea of an ethics based on personal conviction can be understood as a consequence of Kant's theory of moral judgment might be said to show that even if one appeals to the notion of duty, which implies the existence of universally valid ethical norms, it is nevertheless an individual's earnest convictions concerning duty which turn out to be the decisive factor; so that these convictions must themselves be regarded as the highest authority in ethics. If one accepts this view of the matter, we appear to have some form of ethical subjectivism, either a weak or a strong one, depending on the status that one accords these convictions, that is, whether they are considered to be reliable guides concerning duty or merely the expression of certain personal preferences. An alternative approach might be to avoid any appeal whatsoever to the idea of conscience and to claim instead that the only kind of ethical objectivity to which we can appeal is the set of ethical values that just happens to prevail in a particular historical community. This appears to involve the renunciation of the demand for insight into what one holds to be a duty, however, and, given the fact that Hegel views such insight as being integral to the principle of subjective freedom, it is highly unlikely that he would want to endorse such a viewpoint.

At the same time, Hegel clearly wants to avoid ethical subjectivism, as is evident from his description of the true conscience as the disposition to will what is essentially good in the shape of a set of objective determinations and duties; and, since the moral standpoint fails to supply these objective determinations and duties, Hegel claims that the union of subjective knowledge with such an objective system of ethical principles and duties is present only at the standpoint of ethical life (PR §137). In other words, ethical life constitutes a system of universally valid ethical determinations (i.e. laws and institutions) which give rise to various duties while remaining compatible with the principle of subjective freedom, including the right to insight into what one holds to be good or true.

The solution that Hegel thus proposes to the problem as to how subjective freedom can be reconciled with the idea of an objective ethics raises a couple of specific issues in relation to his criticisms of the formal conscience which I need to mention. To begin with, I intend to argue in the final section of the next chapter that Hegel must allow that there will be cases in which personal conviction turns out to be the decisive factor even in relation to the determinations of modern ethical life. This is because he can be seen to hold the view that conscience has a major role to play in modern ethical life, a role that concerns the way in which these ethical determinations, like the moral law, need to be applied. I intend to suggest, moreover, that conscience, as described by Kant and Fichte, exhibits certain qualities that are of particular importance in relation to this role. The qualities in question are those of independent thinking and a sense of personal responsibility. In connection with this last point, we might recall that Kant claims that it is incumbent on an individual to enlighten his understanding with regard to the matter of what is or is not a duty, so as to reduce the possibility of error. Kant in fact sets out stringent conditions concerning what it means to judge in a conscientious way, for he claims that I must not only be of the opinion that what I propose to do is right, but I must also be certain of this (R 186). Kant illustrates this point with the example of an inquisitor, who is presumably firm in his belief that a supernaturally divine will permits him to eradicate all supposed unbelief together with the unbelievers. Kant doubts, however, that the inquisitor could claim to be as strongly convinced of the rightness of what he proposes to do as is required for daring to destroy a human life; and he therefore argues that the inquisitor would be acting unconscientiously if he were to risk doing something that would be wrong to the highest degree (R 186–87).

This demand for absolute certainty raises its own problem, however, because cases in which people experience such an absolute certainty, rather than an earnest conviction which at the same time leaves room for doubt, is arguably very rare indeed. Consequently, if the demand for absolute certainty is taken seriously, it is more likely to give rise to indecision and an inability to act than to lead to the elimination of error. Kant nevertheless stresses the importance of thinking independently and accepting personal responsibility for the decisions that one makes, even if he overstates his case; and I shall argue that these are qualities that Hegel would want the members of the modern state, as presented in his philosophy of right, to possess. In this respect, his theory of modern ethical life will be seen to consist not only of various laws and institutions, but also of certain attitudes, including the kind of disposition which Kant thinks is characteristic of the person who applies the categorical imperative in a conscientious manner.

Another issue concerns the fact that both Kant and Fichte offer theories of right and thus set definite limits to the extent to which appeals to conscience can be used to justify one's actions. We shall see, however, that Hegel's theory of modern ethical life can be understood as a response to the limitations of the conception of right with which both Kant and Fichte operate. The most important of these limitations will be shown to be the way in which this conception of right in Hegel's view fails to properly explain the possibility of an objective ethics which is fully compatible with the idea of moral autonomy, whereas his own theory of right represents an attempt to fully realize this idea. In this respect, although Kant's Copernican Revolution in moral philosophy can be said to consist in his discovery that the law is not a mere restriction on freedom but is itself a product of freedom,[8] he fails, according to Hegel, to fully develop the implications of this insight in relation to the concept of right; and, as we shall see, the reason for this failure is that Kant emphasizes the way in which right limits the exercise of free choice at the expense of the idea of right as a product of human freedom. Hegel, by contrast, seeks to show that the concept of autonomy cannot be realized in an individual's inner world alone but must instead find expression in the social world that he inhabits. He thus attempts to return the positive concept of freedom to the domain of human life from which Kant has been said to have taken it by turning Rousseau's doctrine of a social contract, through which a people comes to govern itself in accordance with laws that spring from its own general will, into a moral and metaphysical doctrine.[9] We shall see, however, that Hegel has some criticisms to make of social contract theory and is thus led to offer a different account of the general will to the one offered by Rousseau.

Before turning to Hegel's theory of modern ethical life and, more specifically, to his attempt to realize the principle of subjective freedom within the latter, I first intend to continue looking at the tension between subjectivity and the idea that there are certain universally valid ethical norms to which we ought to conform, in so far as this tension has, for Hegel, manifested itself in the modern world. Hegel's remarks on Romantic irony in fact suggest that what finally emerges out of the development which subjectivity undergoes in the course of history is the opposite of autonomy of the will, that is, heteronomy of the will, even though the Romantic ironist is someone who makes a point of claiming that he is absolutely free. Subjectivity thus appears to be at odds with itself; for although it retains the aspirations to which Kant's idea of moral autonomy gives rise, it misconstrues this idea and fails to recognize what would constitute its true realization. By considering this problem, we shall also discover Hegel's reason for thinking that negative freedom, which he associates with the arbitrary will or freedom of choice, represents an inadequate conception of freedom.

Romantic Irony

According to Hegel, the formal conscience results in a form of inwardness which 'knows *itself* as that which *wills* and *resolves in a particular way* but may *equally well* will and resolve otherwise', with the result that subjectivity knows itself as the absolute (PR §140A). This form of inwardness finds expression in Romantic irony; and Hegel has two main reasons for including a discussion of this form of irony in his philosophy of right. The first reason is a fairly obvious one, and I shall therefore not spend much time on it, whereas the second one shows why Hegel considers the negative conception of freedom to be inadequate.

In the philosophy of right, Romantic irony represents the final form of evil that has its source in the limitations of the moral standpoint. Hegel considers Romantic irony to be a form of evil because with it subjectivity is explicitly identified as the power determining the content of the good, and this is why he characterizes it as subjectivity which knows itself as the absolute. By proclaiming itself to be absolutely free and the power over everything, Romantic irony appears to reject the notion of a genuinely ethical content of the will; the content of the will is instead made to depend on an arbitrary decision on the part of the subject to adopt one content rather than another as its object and end; a decision which is clearly at odds with the idea of universally valid ethical norms to which each and every subjective will ought to conform. In other words, whereas the formal conscience appeals to the idea of duty, and can thus be regarded as a weak form of ethical subjectivism, Romantic irony involves a complete rejection of this idea and therefore constitutes a strong form of ethical subjectivism.

Hegel compares the Romantic form of irony unfavourably with Socratic irony. He does so because Socrates treated ironically only the unsustainable claims that people would make when questioned by him, such as their inadequate definitions of the good, and, in the case of the Sophists, the claim that they were the teachers of an art, whereas the good itself is not treated ironically (PR §140A). One of the key roles played by Romantic irony in the philosophy of right is therefore to be understood as the way in which it represents the most radical example of a peculiarly modern form of ethical subjectivism, which Hegel thinks can be traced back to the failures of Kantian morality. By stressing the evil character of this peculiarly modern phenomenon in the way that he does, Hegel seeks to make the need for an account of the 'true' conscience appear more pressing.

Hegel claims that this modern form of irony was invented by Friedrich Schlegel and then imitated by others (PK 21). It has been claimed, however, that the type of irony which Schlegel had in mind is closer to Socratic irony than Hegel allows and is also not as immoral as he makes it out to be.[10] Although Hegel possibly misunderstood or misrepresented the theory of irony developed by Schlegel, it is not, in any case, my intention to look more closely at the issue of the allegedly evil character of Romantic irony. I intend to concentrate instead on what I take to be another criticism of it that Hegel is in a position to make, even though he himself does not explicitly make this criticism of Romantic irony. This criticism can be stated independently of the one concerning the evil character of Romantic irony, which, I grant, may rest on a misrepresentation or misunderstanding of Schlegel's conception of irony. Moreover, since modern irony only makes explicit the ethical subjectivism which is already to be found in a weaker form in the claims of the formal conscience, it could be argued that Hegel has established the problem of ethical subjectivism even before he introduces Romantic irony. The criticism which I now intend to discuss relates to the problem of freedom and, what is more, to a conception of freedom which Schlegel himself identifies as characterizing the stance adopted by the Romantic ironist. We shall see that this criticism of modern irony, which can be formulated using some remarks that Hegel makes in his philosophy of right and his lectures on the philosophy of art, undermines the Romantic ironist's claim to be absolutely free.

In his lectures on the philosophy of art, Hegel claims that Romantic irony is the result of the application to art of the principles of Fichte's philosophy, especially the way in which Fichte makes the 'I' into the absolute principle of all knowledge (PK 20). The potential for applying the absolute principle of the 'I' to art is, however, more to be found in Schelling's appropriation of Fichte's theory of the 'I' than in Fichte's own account of the latter. In his account of self-consciousness in the *System of Transcendental Idealism*, Schelling links the concept of the 'I' to the concept of freedom by claiming that the proposition which expresses pure consciousness or self-consciousness, the proposition 'I am', contains no actual predicate, but is instead 'the locus of an infinity of possible predicates'.[11] In other words, the 'I' cannot be identified with any single predicate or set of predicates but is instead unlimited in the sense that it is able to conceive of itself in abstraction from the various predicates which it unites within itself and of which it thus forms the ground of unity. Moreover, since Schelling's account of self-consciousness relates to his deduction of the highest principle of all knowledge, the 'I', which possesses the freedom to choose from among an infinity of possible predicates, is held to be the principle of all reality.

Although Schelling's account of the 'I' might thus far be thought to correspond to Fichte's account of the latter, Schelling also makes explicit the creative potential which the 'I' possesses in virtue of its being the principle of all reality and its having the freedom to choose from an infinity of possible predicates; for, as he himself puts it:

> The eternal, timeless act of self-consciousness, which we call 'I', is that which gives all things existence, and so itself needs no other being to support it; bearing and supporting itself, rather, it appears objectively as eternal becoming, and subjectively as producing without limit.[12]

This conception of the 'I' as that which not only bears and supports itself but also gives all things existence finds an echo in Friedrich Schlegel's association of 'the divine breath of irony' with the mood which 'surveys everything, and rises infinitely above everything that is limited, even above one's own art, virtue or genius'.[13] For this mood of radical detachment appears to require the independence of the 'I' from everything other than itself, thus forcing us to introduce the idea of a limitless subject which, like Schelling's 'I', is the condition of its various determinations.

The absolute status that Schelling accords the 'I', together with its capacity to be limitlessly productive, can also be seen to relate directly to a feature of Romantic irony which Hegel criticizes: the belief that the 'I' or subject is absolute in the sense of its having the ability to bestow value on whatever it pleases and, conversely, to deny things value, so that, as Hegel puts it:

> . . . I can destroy, negate everything in me. I can also destroy anything that has validity for me; everything in me is likewise something that I posit. If we remain at this point, nothing essential survives; I recognize nothing, remain lord and master over everything, for I produce it; it has validity only in so far as I want to posit it, I can just as well randomly destroy it; all that is true, ethical, divine is thus for me mere semblance, without being. (PK 20).

In other words, Romantic irony understands itself as creating values instead of simply conforming to the existing values which are held by other people to be objectively valid. Given this understanding of Romantic irony, it is perhaps not surprising that Hegel should include modern irony among the various forms of evil mentioned in the philosophy of right. However, as I have already mentioned, I do not intend to address the issue as to whether or not Romantic irony can in fact be regarded as a form of evil. The issue at stake instead concerns the kind of freedom which the Romantic ironist claims to enjoy. As we shall now see, the type of freedom in question is one that Hegel considers to be the merely formal type of freedom found in the capacity to exercise free choice.

The way in which Schlegel associates irony with a mood in which the subject is able to survey everything with an air of absolute detachment suggests that he has in mind the type of freedom which Hegel associates with the arbitrary will. For Hegel identifies the latter with the subject's capacity to stand above its content, such as its particular drives, so as to resolve on one object of the will rather than another, so that this content is only a possible one for the 'I', which is therefore in the position to choose between various determinations that it regards as external to itself (PR §14). In short, Hegel identifies the arbitrary will with negative freedom, which consists in the capacity to exercise free choice.

When modern irony is treated not only as a theory of artistic creation but also as a life-view, a significant problem arises in relation to the question as to how free the Romantic ironist really is if the absolute freedom which he claims to enjoy simply consists in his ability to abstract from any given content and contemplate in a detached manner the various possibilities that are thus left open to him. In order to illustrate more clearly what this problem is, I shall turn to the aesthetic life-view as portrayed by Kierkegaard in *Either/Or*, since this will help to show what it means for Romantic irony to be treated as a life-view and how the Romantic ironist comes to think that all value is a product of his own will, with there being no limit to what he might produce in this way. I shall use Kierkegaard's description of the aesthetic life-view to suggest that Hegel is in a position to argue that Romantic irony rests on an inadequate conception of freedom, despite the Romantic ironist's view of himself as someone who possesses an absolute independence of everything except the products of his own thought and will.

Although Kierkegaard is considered to be hostile to Hegelian philosophy, his account of the aesthetic life-view can be seen as relevant to Hegel's criticisms of Romantic irony because his own account of the latter, which provides the basis for his characterization of the aesthetic life-view in *Either/Or*, largely corresponds to Hegel's account of it.[14] For example, in *The Concept of Irony* Kierkegaard claims that this form of irony functioned as 'that for which nothing was established, as that which was finished with everything, and also as that which had the absolute power to do everything'.[15] This characterization of Romantic irony clearly accords with Hegel's view of it as something immoral, as well as with the way in which he associates it with a formal conception of freedom. It is therefore not surprising that, as we shall see, Kierkegaard's portrayal of the aesthetic life-view corresponds to Hegel's description of the Romantic ironist who attempts to live artistically. According to Hegel, this happens when 'what I say, my actions, remain for me a mere show; I give myself a shape, observe this duty; this is posited by me, a shape which I give myself, in relation to which I am not really serious' (PK 21).

In *Either/Or*, Kierkegaard's aesthete employs Hegelian terminology when he mentions a method of overcoming boredom which results in a 'spurious' infinite.[16] A spurious or bad infinite is in Hegel's philosophy an infinite regress or progression, such as is found in the endless division of space and time or the indefinite extension of a numerical series. Another example of a bad infinite is to be found in Hegel's account of desire. At the level of desire, self-consciousness seems to attain an awareness of its absolute power over its object (i.e. that which satisfies its desire) when it destroys the independent object confronting it (e.g. by consuming it) (PhG 143/174). However, if the object were to cease to exist altogether, desire could not be satisfied; and this means that self-consciousness is ultimately tied to its object at the level of desire. Hegel himself describes this situation in terms of the way in which self-consciousness is unable to supersede the object because this object is the condition of its self-certainty (PhG 143/175). Consequently, at the level of desire, there can only be an endless production of both the object of desire and the desire to destroy it.

For Hegel, the mere givenness of the object, which is a constant feature of desire, is also a constant feature of the arbitrary will. The way in which the arbitrary will chooses between various determinations which are held to be external to the willing subject can in fact serve to illustrate a problem which arises when freedom is identified exclusively with negative freedom or freedom of choice. For even though the will is formally free in the sense that it can resolve on one content of the will rather than another, and is universal in virtue of its capacity to abstract from all content, it nevertheless remains dependent on the objects of choice that just happen to be available to it and on the factors that determine it to choose one thing rather than another. We have already encountered this incommensurability between the will's form (i.e. universality) and its content (i.e. the particular and contingent objects of its choice) in Hegel's account of happiness. The fact that this incommensurability is characteristic of the arbitrary will as such leads Hegel to claim that the latter is the will as contradiction and not the will in its truth (PR §15A).

Hegel identifies what exactly this contradiction is when he states that the arbitrary will contains two factors: 'free reflection, which abstracts from everything, and dependence on an inwardly or externally given content and material' (PR §15). In other words, through its capacity to abstract from everything, the will shows itself to be free, but, in its dependency on a given content, whether the latter has to do with external objects or the desires and opinions that determine the choices that the willing subject eventually makes, it shows itself to be unfree. I now intend to use Kierkegaard's characterization of the aesthetic life-view in *Either/Or* to show how the contradiction in question is one to which the Romantic ironist is subject, even though he claims to be absolutely free.

Kierkegaard's aesthete points out that it is possible to change one's immediate surroundings time and again, or to seek distraction after distraction outside oneself, without ever fully overcoming boredom; and this brings to mind the way in which the satisfaction of desire requires the endless perpetuation of its object. The reason that the individual is unable to fully overcome boredom by these means is that it is always possible for the feeling of boredom to reassert itself in such cases, so that new means will be required to conquer it again. It might, for instance, become necessary to seek ever more distant or unfamiliar places in which to live or to visit, or ever more powerful forms of distraction. In other words, the conditions tend to perpetuate themselves in such attempts to overcome boredom. This leads Kierkegaard's aesthete to advocate an intensive, rather than extensive, type of change, which involves transforming experience poetically through one's having perfected the art of remembering and forgetting; an art which rests on the following principle: 'No part of life ought to have so much meaning for a person that he cannot forget it any moment he wants to; on the other hand, every single part of life ought to have so much meaning for a person that he can remember it at any moment'.[17]

Kierkegaard's aesthete claims that in order to develop the ability to determine the importance of each life-situation, an individual must maintain a certain distance from people and events, since too deep an involvement with anything or anybody would make it difficult for him to determine the amount of significance which he attaches to things. The aesthete therefore advises against marrying and forming close friendships, and instead recommends taking delight in that which is purely accidental, such as a chance encounter with a woman or a peculiarity that another person just happens to exhibit. While this lack of genuine commitment to such forms of the ethical as friendship and marriage indicates why Kierkegaard, like Hegel, thinks that Romantic irony is immoral, the issue that we need to address concerns the question as to whether or not the aesthete is as absolutely free as he makes himself out to be.

As we have seen, the aesthete's absolute freedom consists in his ability to determine the level of importance that he attaches to something, so that he is able to remember or forget it at will. This in turn depends on his capacity to choose between various life-situations, some of which, such as marriage and the forming of close friendships, would threaten his ability to remember or forget at will, whereas other more trivial life-situations do not carry the same kind of commitment, and consequently do not involve the same level of risk. The aesthete's aim can therefore be characterized as the wish to maintain maximal freedom of choice; and the importance that he thus attaches to the capacity for freedom of choice allows us to identify the type of freedom in question with the negative concept of freedom that Hegel associates with the arbitrary will; a form of freedom which also has a significant role to play in Schlegel's theory of irony. This invites the question as to whether or not the aesthete is subject to the same contradiction to which Hegel thinks the arbitrary will is subject.

I would argue that the contradiction in the arbitrary will between the form of the will (i.e. universality) and its content is indeed also present in the case of the aesthetic life-view. For a start, the aesthete ultimately relies on external events to provide the content of his reflections, so that he is dependent on the continual existence of situations whose significance he is allegedly able to determine. Since this content is taken from what is purely accidental, the supply of 'interesting' situations might, however, dry up, or the individual who practises this form of reflection might eventually grow bored and disenchanted with it, and will thus be forced to seek other forms of distraction. In this respect, the aesthete appears subject to a number of factors that lie beyond his control. Moreover, the aesthetic life-view appears subject to other conditions, such as the fact that the aesthete's ability to determine the level of importance that he attaches to things appears to rest on a peculiar talent, which he might not have possessed in the first place and which he might not possess in the future.

Since he is subject to all these conditions, the individual who adopts the aesthetic life-view cannot in fact be said to enjoy an absolute freedom. He is, in fact, determined by the experiences and situations that happen to be available to him, and he is dependent on the possession of a talent which he just happens to possess but might not possess in the future. In the first case, the aesthetic life-view appears to be conditioned by the existence of the object of his reflections in the same way as desire is conditioned by its object, which forms the condition of its satisfaction; so that the aesthete's distinction between intensive and extensive types of change turns out to be an essentially meaningless one. While the aesthete's gift for being able to determine the level of importance that he attaches to things appears to reduce his freedom to what are arguably the most given of all forms of determinations, namely, natural ones.

Hegel claims that the arbitrary will involves an illusion because the person who considers himself to be free makes something particular into what counts for him but does not reflect on the fact that this particular content is a merely given one; and this leads him to add that it is often when they are to the greatest extent subject to external forms of determination that people believe themselves to act most freely (VRP 3 137). In other words, people commonly consider themselves to be free because they possess the capacity to choose one thing rather than another; yet these same people fail to recognize that their capacity to choose is limited by the choices available to them and the other factors which determine the actual choices that they make. It appears that what Hegel here has to say about the arbitrary will is equally true of the Romantic ironist's claim to be absolutely free.

Kierkegaard also recognizes the illusory nature of the Romantic ironist's claim to be absolutely free, for he states that 'the ironist, who considers himself free, thereby falls under the horrible law of world irony and drudges along in the most frightful slavery'.[18] As I have shown, this is a claim that Hegel could also have made. If he had done so, it would have been easier to identify another function that his remarks on Romantic irony have in his philosophy of right: the function of showing the need for a more adequate conception of freedom, which is what Hegel himself seeks to provide with his theory of modern ethical life. He would also have been able to offer a criticism of a conception of freedom which is not restricted to Romantic irony alone. Indeed, the wider significance of the argument that I have constructed using Hegel's remarks on Romantic irony and the arbitrary will is evident from the way in which this conception of freedom arguably finds its clearest expression today in consumerism,[19] which can be seen as a natural consequence of identifying freedom exclusively with freedom of choice.

Consumerism can be understood as similar to Romantic irony because it appears to be based on a conception of absolute freedom which can be characterized as an unlimited capacity for making arbitrary choices; yet it really involves a relation of dependency, since it ultimately makes individuals reliant on what is merely given and contingent, such as the individual's particular desires and preferences and that which promises to satisfy them. Consumerism therefore makes individuals dependent on forces that remain beyond their control. It is, I believe, possible to credit Hegel with providing us with the resources for unmasking the contradictory nature of this conception of freedom which finds expression in both consumerism and Romantic irony, and appears to reduce the idea of freedom to a matter of personal idiosyncrasy.

Although Hegel considers the negative freedom of the arbitrary will to be deficient in comparison to the form of freedom which announces itself in the idea of moral autonomy, he thinks that it must nevertheless be accommodated within his theory of modern ethical life, and we have already encountered two reasons for this: the fact that freedom of choice constitutes the bare possibility of autonomy and the fact that each person is able to determine himself as an individual through the exercise of free choice. It is therefore now time to turn to Hegel's theory of modern ethical life and his attempt to realize within it the various rights that fall under the principle of subjective freedom, which will be seen to include the right to exercise free choice. I shall begin with Hegel's theory of civil society, since this is the sphere of modern ethical life in which he seeks to realize most of the rights that fall under the principle of subjective freedom. Civil society is therefore of the utmost importance in relation to what I take to be the central aim of Hegel's philosophy of right: the aim of situating subjectivity in the sense of integrating it into a set of universally valid ethical determinations that are compatible with the principle of subjective freedom.

Chapter 3: Modern Ethical Life

Civil Society and the Arbitrary Will

One of the main ways in which civil society realizes the principle of subjective freedom concerns its function of accommodating the particularity of the will, in the shape of the individual's specific needs, desires and arbitrary will, within modern ethical life. Civil society is, in short, the sphere of modern ethical life in which the subject's right to experience the satisfaction of its particularity is realized. The individual therefore enters civil society as the 'concrete person who, as a *particular* person, as a totality of needs and a mixture of natural necessity and arbitrariness [*Willkür*], is his own end' (PR §182). In other words, the individual enters civil society as a being with certain basic needs, such as the need for food, drink, clothing and shelter, along with other non-natural needs and certain opinions regarding how these needs are to be satisfied; and it is within civil society that this particular individual seeks to satisfy these needs. The individual thus enters civil society as a person who makes his own particular will into the end of his activity, so that in civil society the principle of self-interest is posited (VRP 2 147).

The individual's needs are not restricted to his most basic natural needs because human beings, unlike animals, are capable of multiplying and refining their needs, along with the means of satisfying them, which in turn become needs (PR §§190–91). The way in which civil society accommodates this multiplication and refinement of needs is evidence of the extent to which it allows free play to the particularity of the will, in the shape of opinion and caprice, since these non-natural needs are of an essentially contingent nature. Hegel therefore describes civil society as the sphere of ethical life in which everything particular has free play (VRP 2 149). Moreover, even the satisfaction of an individual's most basic needs becomes a matter of free choice in civil society because there is a range of possible means of satisfying them (e.g. different types of food or clothing). Since the negative concept of freedom which Hegel identifies with the arbitrary will in this way finds its rightful place in civil society, the latter must be seen as the sphere of modern ethical life in which human beings come to distinguish themselves from others through the exercise of free choice, so that the differences between them are not merely natural ones but are instead products of their own subjective wills.

In addition to the satisfaction of particular needs, Hegel describes another way in which the arbitrary will is allowed to express itself in civil society, which this time concerns the type of work that an individual does. Hegel claims that in modern ethical life individuals freely choose to enter a trade or other occupation, even though one's choice of work will be limited by such factors as natural ability or talent and one's level of education; and he therefore thinks that the question as to which class (*Stand*) an individual belongs also becomes a matter of opinion and free choice, since in choosing to enter a particular trade or occupation, one at the same time chooses to enter a certain class (PR §206). This is why Hegel claims that the principle of subjective particularity is denied its rights by Plato, who assigns to the rulers of the state the task of choosing the class to which each individual belongs (PR §206A).

The fact that individuals are given the opportunity to pursue their own personal ends, which are, by their very nature, ones that they have an inclination to pursue, also means that the right to identify with the objects of one's concern through having an incentive or inclination to pursue the ends that one does is realized in civil society. Civil society can thus already be seen to realize two of the rights that fall under the principle of subjective freedom, namely, the right of subjective freedom and the right of the subjective will.

The multiplication and refinement of needs and the means of satisfying them mentioned above has an unintended consequence, however; one that to some extent counterbalances the self-interest which otherwise animates civil society. This unintended consequence concerns the fact that the work performed in order to produce and provide the commodities that will satisfy the needs of civil society becomes ever more particularized, with each person's activity becoming restricted to a specific task, so that the members of civil society become ever more dependent on each other for the satisfaction of their needs (PR §198). The individual therefore also enters civil society as someone who relies on others for the satisfaction of his needs and helps to satisfy the needs of others. Since each person acquires the means for the satisfaction of his needs from others, he must take into consideration their opinions, and, conversely, since that which each person produces or provides is determined by the needs of others, it only makes sense to produce or provide goods for which there is a demand (PR §192Z). A kind of universality thus arises which consists in the quality of being recognized, so that particular needs, together with the means of satisfying them, take on a social dimension (PR §192). The way in which self-interest gives rise, albeit in an unconscious fashion, to a more universalistic state of affairs leads Hegel to identify the form of universality as another principle of civil society (PR §182), even though he elsewhere claims that subjective particularity is its animating principle (PR §206A).

This condition of mutual dependence, which Hegel calls the system of needs, means that each individual's well-being becomes bound up with the well-being of others (PR §183). The system of needs can therefore be seen as the sphere of modern ethical life in which the idea of the welfare of all, which at the level of morality remains an abstraction, finds its realization. Indeed, Hegel's description of the welfare of all sounds very much like his description of the system of needs; for he describes it as a condition in which no one can seek to promote his own welfare without at the same time either consciously or unconsciously promoting the welfare of others, so that 'no one can eat or drink without this benefiting others' (VRP 4 334). As we shall see, the common interest which arises in this way has a significant role to play in Hegel's philosophy of right, for he considers it to be an integral feature of the modern state. On the other hand, he argues against identifying the essence of ethical life with such a common interest, and, as we shall see, this leads him to offer a theory of right which represents an alternative to the modern natural law tradition, even though it also draws heavily from this tradition.

The universal dimension to civil society relates to Hegel's aim of providing an ethics, since the quality of being recognized extends beyond the satisfaction of needs to include social norms which have their ultimate basis in the system of needs. To begin with, the condition of mutual dependence which characterizes the latter gives rise to shared practices and common patterns of behaviour that serve to link individuals more closely together. Hegel cites as an example of this process the way in which it becomes necessary for individuals to follow certain conventions concerning such matters as how one dresses and the time of day at which one eats one's meals (PR §192Z). Hegel's point is that if someone wants to fulfil his particular purposes, he must conform to the accepted norms that characterize the system in which these purposes can be best realized. Individuals can, in short, attain their own personal ends only in so far as they think and act in conformity with these norms (PR §187). In this respect, civil society can be held to perform the function of teaching human beings to limit their own activity, which, as we saw, forms a condition of individuality in the sense that a person can determine himself as an individual only if others grant him a sphere in which to exercise free choice. This means that the discipline which makes such self-limitation possible need not assume the form of a master-slave relationship in the modern state, whereas Hegel thinks that it must assume this form, or one similar to it, in the state of nature.

The need to conform to society's norms so as to realize one's own personal ends and purposes means that far from being the sphere in which one's individuality is fully expressed, civil society turns out to be the kind of environment in which it is necessary to suppress one's particularity, that is to say, the kind of environment in which, as Kierkegaard puts it, 'a self is the last thing the world cares about and the most dangerous thing of all for a person to show signs of having'.[1] Hegel admittedly also mentions the need to distinguish oneself from others as another feature of civil society (PR §193); and an example of this is to be found in the drive to gain worth as this particular person by competing with others (VRP 1 114). Moreover, in certain cases, the wish to distinguish oneself from others is inextricably linked with the wish to imitate others. Hegel cites fashion as an example of this phenomenon because it involves the following process: 'One imitates others, and this is the origin of fashion; one wants to have what the others have, but once one has achieved this, one is then not satisfied; one wants to have something special. Then others copy this and thus it goes on endlessly' (VRP 4 491). The example of fashion suggests, however, that even if the desire to distinguish oneself from others is a feature of civil society, Hegel thinks that the tendency towards conformity nevertheless continually asserts itself, so that the act of determining oneself as an individual and recognition of the fact that one is of the same general type as others come to form part of the same process.

As we saw in Chapter 1, the determination of oneself as an individual distinct from others and one's awareness of being of the same general type as others relate to the two aspects of subjectivity that for Hegel are unified in the concept of personality, while this concept can itself only be realized within the universal self-consciousness of spirit. Consequently, we can think of individuals in civil society as becoming persons through being made to behave in ways that accord with the idea of spirit, even though their thoughts and actions do not necessarily proceed from an explicit understanding of themselves as members of this universal self-consciousness. In this respect, Hegel must be seen to view the suppression of particularity which takes place in civil society as having a positive role to play in modern ethical life. Hegel characterizes this role in more general terms as educating subjectivity in its particularity (*die Subjektivität in ihrer Besonderheit zu bilden*) (PR §187), so that civil society can be understood as representing an important stage in the development of that which Hegel calls culture (*Bildung*), which he describes as acting and behaving in a universal manner (VRP 4 483).

Another feature of Hegel's account of civil society which will be shown to be highly significant in relation to his attempt to fully incorporate the principle of subjective freedom into his philosophy of right concerns the way in which he links civil society with a particular conception of right; for although the social norms described above arise in an unconscious manner, the common interest that develops on the basis of the system of needs requires a set of publicly known laws that can be applied and enforced by the relevant authorities. These laws, which must be consciously produced, relate to the way in which civil society serves to accommodate the arbitrary will within Hegel's theory of modern ethical life because many of them are designed to protect the formal freedom of persons, which mainly consists in the freedom to do as one pleases just so long as one does not violate the right of others to do the same. This implies the conception of right which finds expression in Kant's 'universal law of right', which he defines as follows: so act externally that the free use of your choice [*Willkür*] can coexist with the freedom of everyone in accordance with a universal law (MS 231). This leads Kant to describe right in general as 'the sum of the conditions under which the choice of one can be united with the choice of another in accordance with a universal law of freedom' (MS 230). Hegel claims in relation to Kant's definition of right that it contains 'only a *negative* determination – that of limitation' (PR §29A); and we shall see that he does so because right is here understood primarily as setting limits to freedom of choice.

Civil society realizes Kant's universal law of right, which for Hegel finds expression in the demand to be a person and respect others as persons (PR §36), through its laws and the legal system which applies them, as well as through the public authority (*die Polizei*), whose main tasks include law enforcement. Both the legal system and the public authority are necessary because the effectiveness of the universal law of right depends on the existence of institutions which seek to protect the rights of all persons, irrespective of the particular needs, desires, opinions and interests that serve to distinguish one person from another person. The legal system also recognizes the right of individuals to be held responsible only for those actions that they intended and those consequences that they could have reasonably foreseen as resulting from their actions, so that civil society realizes the right of knowledge.

While the legal system serves to realize the universal law of right, the public authority not only enforces the particular laws deriving from this universal law but also regulates the market economy which arises on the basis of the system of needs, so that it functions effectively and in everyone's interests (PR §§235, 236).[2] This shows that although Hegel thinks that freedom of trade and commerce is necessary if an individual's activity is to be mediated by his arbitrary will and his particular interests, as is required by the right of subjective freedom, he at the same time accepts that some level of state intervention will be necessary. I shall now say something more about this need for state intervention in order to explain the transition from civil society to the political state, which forms the third and final moment of Hegel's theory of modern ethical life and comprises the constitutional monarch, who symbolizes the state's sovereignty, the legislature and the executive (PR §273).

The need for state intervention relates to the inner dialectic which drives civil society beyond itself, as when, for example, it is led to seek new markets abroad on account of the problem of overproduction, which occurs when the volume of goods produced lacks a corresponding number of consumers (PR §§246, 248Z), with colonization being the logical outcome of this process because it provides new markets and a new sphere of industrial activity for its members (PR §248). Colonization, which thus represents an attempt to resolve the inner dialectic of civil society, also provides an example of the need for a power which concerns itself with the universal interest as such, as opposed to particular interests, whether those of individual persons or of any group of individuals within society. For this attempt to resolve the inner dialectic of civil society demands considerable resources, and such resources could arguably be more easily provided and more effectively employed by the state than by private individuals. Hegel himself appears to make the same point when he makes a distinction between sporadic and systematic forms of colonization (PR §248Z). The necessity of the political state is also demonstrated by the way in which the legal system applies laws and the public authority enforces them, as well as putting various regulations into effect; for these laws and regulations presuppose the existence of an authority whose task is to formulate them and decide on the best ways of implementing them. Consequently, Hegel claims that the confusion which arises in civil society can be restored to harmony only through state intervention (PR §185Z), by which he means the political state, which, as previously mentioned, forms the final moment of his theory of modern ethical life.

As it stands, Hegel's account of the transition from civil society to the political state appears to rest on the demand for a universal power which is independent of the particular interests governing civil society. The systematic function of civil society in his philosophy of right can therefore be identified with the way in which it allows Hegel to offer a proof of the necessity of a universal which has power over all that is merely particular.[3] This argument is based on the idea that the necessity of the political state is demonstrated by the fact that only it can prevent civil society from destroying itself through the unlimited extension of its own principle, which is the principle of self-interest.

Although I think it is wrong to claim that this is the only systematic function of civil society, since the latter also serves to realize three of the rights that fall under the principle of subjective freedom and will later be seen to partially realize the fourth one (i.e. the right of the subjective will to recognize nothing as good or true that it does not perceive as rational), this interpretation of the transition from civil society to the political state succeeds in capturing an essential feature of the relation of civil society to the political state. Herbert Marcuse might therefore seem justified in claiming both that civil society for Hegel generates an 'authoritarian system' and that an 'uncontrovertible [sic] authority' must be imposed on the individual interests animating it.[4] This characterization of the relation of civil society to the state suggests that the latter will appear highly oppressive to the members of civil society. Yet Marcuse's view of the relation of the political state to civil society must be seen as a mistaken one for two main reasons.

To begin with, civil society is the sphere of ethical life in which the right of the subject to experience the satisfaction of its particularity finds its realization and, as we have seen, this requires a sphere of ethical life in which individuals can effectively exercise free choice without interference from others. Since the effective exercise of free choice also requires that individuals limit their activity in relation to each other, it would be inconsistent of Hegel to claim that the state has an unlimited right to impose itself upon the subjective wills of its citizens other than in exceptional circumstances (e.g. in the event of war). Secondly, we have seen that for Hegel the members of civil society come to adopt a more universalistic standpoint as a result of their need to cooperate with each other, so that the gap between particular interests and the universal interest, which is embodied in the political state, has to a large extent already been bridged.

In connection with the last point, it has been claimed that in civil society the *bourgeois* learns to be a citizen.[5] Although this claim is, I believe, closer to the truth than Marcuse's characterization of the relation of civil society to the state, it misconstrues Hegel's actual position as well. Hegel associates the citizen (*Bürger*) as *bourgeois* specifically with civil society (PR §190A); and he describes the *bourgeois* as a private person (VRP 2

150), that is to say, someone who is concerned with the satisfaction of his needs and lacks any political relation, unlike the *citoyen* (VRP 4 472). In the next chapter, we shall see that Hegel holds the view that it is possible for someone who participates in the most universalistic aspect of civil society (i.e. the corporation) to remain an essentially private person; and there is consequently a problem with the idea that the *bourgeois* becomes a *citoyen* merely through his participation in civil society.

Moreover, although for Hegel civil society involves the adoption of more universalistic ways of thinking and acting and requires the intervention of the political state, the conception of the state that we thus arrive at does not for Hegel correspond to the true essence of ethical life. The inadequacy of this conception of the state concerns the kind of relation between the subjective will of the individual and the universal will, as embodied in the laws and institutions of the state, that it implies; a relation which, as we shall see, is considered by Hegel to be incommensurate with the positive concept of freedom found in Kant's idea of moral autonomy, even though it accords with his aim of subordinating the subjective will to the universal will. According to Hegel, the reason for this incommensurability is that the conception of the state as a universal which has power over all that is merely particular turns the relation of the universal will to the subjective will into a merely external one, whereas the positive concept of freedom expressed in the idea of moral autonomy establishes an identity between them, as is the case with Kant's notion of a self-legislating pure practical reason, in which the moral subject legislates the laws which it obeys. In order to illustrate this idea of a merely external relation between the universal will and the subjective will of the individual, I now intend to turn to some criticisms that Hegel makes of social contract theory, which he accuses of confusing the state with civil society, and to then relate these criticisms to Fichte's contract theory of the state in particular, which, Hegel claims, turns the relation between the subjective will and the universal will into a merely external one. In this way, I also hope to give some idea of the unity of the subjective will and the universal will which is for Hegel constitutive of modern ethical life.

Hegel's Critique of Fichte's Contract Theory of the State

For Hegel, the identity of the subjective will and the universal will demanded by the moral standpoint can only be realized at the level of ethical life; and he accordingly describes the ethical relation as the identity of the particular will and the universal will (VRP 2 124). The 'abstract' concept of ethical life is therefore 'the unity of the subjective and objective will, the universality of the will as identical with the subjectivity of the will' (VRP 4 395). As I have already mentioned, Hegel does not think that the unity of the subjective will and the universal will is fully realized at the level of civil society. His reasons for thinking this become clearer if we look at some of his main criticisms of social contract theory, especially as they relate to Fichte's version of it.

As we shall see, in Hegel's view contract theories of the state ultimately end up identifying the state with that which serves to protect and promote the interests of its individual members, with the result that the state is accorded the status of a means to an end. As with Hegel's account of civil society, such a conception of the state may take as its point of departure the fact that individuals are brought together when they realize that they depend on each other for the satisfaction of their needs. As we shall see below, this is in fact precisely the way in which Hegel views Rousseau's version of the social contract, which he takes to be based on the idea of a common interest. Admittedly, neither Hegel nor the social contract theorists whom he criticizes identify civil society simply with a condition of mutual dependence since, in addition to what Hegel calls the system of needs, civil society includes other elements, such as the legal system and the public authority, while these institutions in turn presuppose the political state in its legislative and executive functions. It could nevertheless be argued that these institutions arise later in order to protect and further the common interest which first manifests itself at the level of the system of needs. Alternatively, social contract theory can take the need to preserve one's life and secure one's property as its point of departure, and, as we shall see, this is the case with Fichte's version of it. Hegel rejects both these conceptions of the state, however, on the grounds that the interests of individuals as such are made into the ultimate end for which they are united (PR §258A). In Hegel's view, this amounts to confusing the state, by which, for reasons given below, he means a unified political community, with civil society, which has its foundation and starting-point in the particular interests of its individual members (VRP 4 472). In this respect, social contract theory succeeds in comprehending the essence of civil society and its relation to the political state while failing to comprehend the essence of ethical life.

Although Hegel associates Rousseau with a conception of the state which confuses the latter with civil society (PR §29A), he praises him for making the will into the principle of the state (PR §258A). Indeed, we shall see that Hegel, like Rousseau, understands the state to be an expression of the general will and as deriving its legitimacy from this fact. However, although he praises Rousseau for making a distinction between the general will (*la volonté générale*) and the will of all (*la volonté de tous*), Hegel accuses him of failing to maintain this distinction (EL §163Z1). For Rousseau, the general will is meant to be something more than the will of all; for whereas the general will pays attention only to the common interest, the will of all, which is no more than a sum total of particular wills (*une somme de volontés particulieres*), is based on private interests.[6] In the light of Hegel's account of civil society, we may ask whether this distinction between the general will and the will of all can be maintained. For in civil socity the pursuit of private interest gives rise to a common interest in the sense that individuals are made to recognize that their own interests are best served through cooperation; and they consequently become willing to accept the imposition of limitations, in the shape of laws and regulations, on their freedom of choice.

The common interest which arises when individuals come to accept that their needs and interests can be better satisfied in a law-governed condition than in a state of nature is, for Hegel, a deficient form of universality, however; one that does not express the true nature of ethical life. This is evident from his claim that a condition of general well-being (*allgemeine Wohl*) would not yet be the state, since all that we would then have is a collection of individuals (*ein Kollektivum*) but not universality (*die Allgemeinheit*) (VRP 4 338). I shall now turn to Fichte's contract theory of the state which serves to give a better idea of Hegel's main reasons for claiming that the universality which is characteristic of the common good or interest is a deficient form of universality.

According to Hegel, Fichte, like Rousseau, makes the mistake of considering the will only in 'the determinate form of the *individual* will' (PR §258A). We shall see that this leads Fichte to commit another of Rousseau's errors, which is to regard the universal will 'only as the *common element* [*das Gemeinschaftliche*] arising out of this individual will *as a conscious will*' (PR §258A), even though Fichte seeks to attribute to the state a type of universality that differs from the type of universality which arises through the combination of many individual wills. In Hegel's view, Fichte fails to achieve this aim because he cannot explain the unity of the subjective will and the universal will, but instead turns their relation to each other into a purely external one.

Fichte employs a transcendental argument in his *Foundations of Natural Right* to demonstrate the necessity of the state, and in so doing he appeals to the idea of a contract between private persons. While Hegel restricts the making of contracts to an agreement between persons concerning the alienation of property, Fichte puts forward the theory of a civil contract, which consists of various stages, with each successive stage proving to be a necessary condition of the application of the previous stage.

To begin with, there is the citizens' property contract. This contract consists in each individual reaching an agreement with all other individuals to respect each other's property rights (GNR 196). However, in order to guarantee the efficacy of such a contract, and to thereby ensure that each individual is not dependent on the good will of others, Fichte argues that it is necessary to make an additional contract, which he terms the protection contract (GNR 197). This second stage turns the merely negative relation of each individual will to every other will into a positive one, since each individual not only agrees to refrain from interfering with the property of others, but also promises to help protect everyone else's property against possible violation by any third party (GNR 198).

This second contract raises an apparently insoluble problem, however: for while it is easy to tell whether the property contract is being fulfilled, since it only requires that at all times others do not interfere with my property and that I do not interfere with theirs, the protection contract cannot be fulfilled at all times, but instead relates to an unforeseeable, and possibly non-existent, event in the future. Each individual cannot, therefore, be certain that other individuals will actually fulfil the obligations that the protection contract imposes upon them. Indeed, each individual is for this very reason justified in refusing to protect the property of others: for I am only bound to protect you under the condition that you protect me, which means that if you are not at present fulfilling this condition, then I am under no obligation to help you (GNR 200). In short, a vicious circle arises, of the type identified by Hobbes, for whom contracts that rely on the relevant parties trusting each other instead of fulfilling their obligations immediately are void in the state of nature.[7] To solve this problem, Fichte introduces that which he terms the unification contract (GNR 204). This contract involves the establishment of a protective power to which each individual on entering the state must agree to contribute by voting to appoint magistrates, paying taxes, and so on (GNR 205).

Fichte thinks that this positing of a protective power not only demonstrates the necessity of the state, but also leads to the establishment of a common will (*gemeinsamer Wille*), as opposed to a merely private one (GNR 203). He justifies this claim on the grounds that, in the case of the unification contract, the individual contracts not with a single individual but with every individual, since it can never be known in advance which specific individual will need protection. Consequently, in order to be certain of receiving protection if one should need it, each individual must, in the face of such ignorance, agree to form part of a whole which includes all other individuals as well as oneself. Fichte claims that this requirement allows us to understand the essential nature of the state in the following way:

> This indeterminacy, this uncertainty as to which individual will first be transgressed against – therefore this *oscillation* in the imagination – is the real bond that unites the different individuals. It is by means of this that all merge together into one, no longer united in just an abstract concept (as a *compositum*), but rather in actuality (as a *totum*). Thus in the state, nature re-unites what she had previously separated when she produced several individuals. Reason is one, and it is exhibited in the sensible world also as one; humanity is a single organized and organizing whole of reason (GNR 203).

It is clear from this passage that although in the earlier stages of his argument Fichte views the state primarily in terms of that which serves to protect the interests of its individual members, he nevertheless wants to ascribe to it a different type of universality from that which arises through an aggregation of individual wills joined together by the bonds of self-interest. The type of universality in question is characteristic of a totality, as is evident from the way in which Fichte goes on to compare the state to an organized product of nature, by which he means something that must be understood in teleological rather than mechanical terms, in the sense of exhibiting an internal purposiveness, with its parts serving to produce the whole, which is itself the end for which its various members are united (GNR 203). It remains unclear, however, as to why Fichte should think that his contract theory of the state implies a *totum*, in which the whole and the parts form a self-producing totality, rather than a *compositum*, which first arises through a combination of its various parts.

One reason for doubting that Fichte has demonstrated that the state must be viewed as a totality is that even though individuals may recognize that they themselves might need protecting, they nevertheless remain free to decide whether or not to take the risk involved in not agreeing to the establishment of a protective power, which they must help to maintain through the payment of taxes. Admittedly, the consequences of making such a decision may well be enough to deter anyone from taking this risk. The possibility of making the decision not to agree to the establishment of a protective power remains, however, a real one in the case of Fichte's contract theory of the state. Indeed, in the following passage Fichte himself admits that membership of the state is ultimately an optional matter:

> Now in the doctrine of right there is no talk of moral obligation; each is bound only by the free, arbitrary [*willkürlichen*] decision to live in community with others, and if someone does not at all want to limit his free choice [*Willkür*], then within the field of the doctrine of right, one can say nothing further against him, other than that he must then remove himself from all human community (GNR 11).

Fichte's contract theory of the state can in this way be seen to relate to the criticism that social contract theory appears to make the union of individuals within the state depend on these same individuals' arbitrary wills and opinions (PR §258A). This in turn means that the relation of the subjective will of the individual to the universal will embodied in the laws and institutions of the state is an essentially contingent one.

The way in which the relation of the subjective will to the universal will remains an essentially contingent one in Fichte's contract theory of the state makes it incompatible with the idea of a totality, which is not only produced by its parts but also determines their relation both to itself and to each other, so that the whole and the parts form a single unified whole and thus stand in an essential relation to each other. The fact that Fichte's contract theory of the state implies a contingent, and thus inessential, relation between the subjective will and the universal will is not, however, the only thing that renders the analogy with an organized product of nature problematic. For it implies that the state is formed through the combination of the subjective wills of those individuals who decide that it is in their best interests to agree to the establishment and maintenance of a protective power which protects their own persons and property. Yet this is clearly at odds with the idea of a totality, which, rather than first being constituted through the combination of many individual parts, requires instead that we think of the whole as being logically prior to its parts.

Fichte's failure to explain how the state constitutes a totality, in which the subjective will and the universal will are properly unified, relates to a specific criticism that Hegel makes of Fichte's theory of right, a criticism which turns on the idea that Fichte comprehends the state merely as an external order (VRP 2 190–91). When Hegel speaks of an external order he has in mind the idea of the state as a protective power, in which the subjective will and the universal will are not properly unified but stand instead in a contingent relation to each other. This external relation of the universal will to the subjective will leads Hegel to speak of the 'external' state or 'state of necessity [*Notstaat*]', which he explicitly identifies with civil society (PR §183). The 'external' state is therefore to be thought of as one in which the relation of the subjective will to the universal will has the appearance of being merely the means by which the individual is able to satisfy his needs (VRP 4 416). Individuals consequently think of themselves as living in a state only as a matter of necessity (VRP 4 474), and they choose to act in an orderly and law-abiding manner only because they realize that they could not otherwise achieve their own ends (VRP 4 481).

Another example of the external relation between the universal will and the subjective will of the individual that is found in the state of necessity relates to the public authority, whose role Hegel describes as an 'external welfare [*Sorge*]' and an 'external order' (VRP 2 152). He describes the role of the public authority in these terms because the latter intervenes in the workings of civil society so as to regulate the economy or preserve public order, thus asserting the primacy of the common interest over all particular interests that threaten it; yet even though it limits their arbitrary wills, individuals accept that such state intervention is necessary because they recognize that their private interests are better served by it than by its absence, as in the state of nature. This conception of the state clearly corresponds to Fichte's account of it as a protective power; and, like the latter, the state of necessity turns out to involve a contingent relation between the subjective will and the universal will, a relation that depends on individuals being of the opinion that it is in their best interests to live in a society governed by law.

A final example of the external relation between the universal will and the subjective will which characterizes the state of necessity consists in the way in which the subjective will of the individual is merely subsumed under the universal will as embodied in law, rather than its being genuinely united with the latter. This subsumption of the subjective will under the universal will is exemplified by the legal system, which applies the laws to which all members of civil society are subject. The relation of the subjective will to the universal will is once again a contingent one because the individual who is found to be guilty of a crime and punished accordingly might have acted in compliance with the law, in which case his subjective will would never have come into relation with the universal will under which it is subsumed.

Hegel's *Natural Law* essay shows that he clearly thinks that Fichte reduces the relation of the universal will to the subjective will to a merely external one. In this essay, Hegel speaks of an opposition between the 'real consciousness', that is, the subject and individual freedom, and that which he describes variously as pure self-consciousness, pure unity, the empty law of ethics and the universal freedom of all (NR 471/132). The opposition in question might equally be expressed as an opposition between the subjective will of the individual and the universal will, as I now intend to show.

Hegel claims that the opposition mentioned above finds expression in Fichte's theory of right in the presupposition that 'honesty [*Treu*] and trust [*Glauben*] are lost' (NR 471/132).[8] This is a direct reference to a passage in Fichte's *Foundations of National Right* in which he introduces that which he terms the law of coercion [*das Zwanggesetz*] (GNR 142), which he describes as a power that 'is posited as a means for establishing mutual security when honesty [*Treue*] and trust [*Glauben*] do not exist' (GNR 146). According to Fichte, this coercive power is necessary because even if freedom and security could prevail as a result of honesty and trust amongst persons, there is no law according to which honesty and trust can be produced (GNR 142). In other words, the fact that individuals act in an honest manner and are therefore genuinely deserving of one's trust is a contingent affair, so that a reluctance to rely solely on the good will of others must be considered fully justified. This lack of assurance regarding the will of another person can in turn only be remedied by the positing of a power which is independent of each and every particular will.[9] This power is the common will, which, in order to preserve itself, must itself be equipped with a power in relation to which the power of each individual is infinitely small. Fichte calls this power the state power, which includes two elements: 'the right to judge, and the right to execute the judgments it has made' (GNR 153). In other words, the law of coercion presupposes the political state in its executive function. Moreover, if the state authority is to be effective, a link must exist between this executive power and the citizens of the state, and the link in question is formed by the public authority (*die Polizei*) (GNR 291–92).

In his *Natural Law* essay, Hegel argues that Fichte in this way presupposes an absolute opposition between the subjective will and the universal will which makes their unification impossible, since the oneness of the will of the individual with the universal will 'cannot be understood and posited as inner absolute majesty', but only as 'something to be produced by an external relation, or by coercion' (NR 472/132). This means, in effect, that Fichte's theory of right fails to show how the subjective will can understand itself as standing in an essential relation to the universal will, as is required by the idea of moral autonomy.[10]

This lack of an essential relation between the subjective will and the universal will is, for Hegel, characteristic of civil society; and this is why he describes the latter as the 'stage of difference' (PR §181), thus associating it with the Doctrine of Essence of his logic, in which two thought-determinations are not grasped as moments of the same totality, even though they appear to stand in an essential relation to each other, so that thought 'assumes the distinctions as *independent* and at the same time posits their relationality *as well*' (EL §114A). In civil society, the subjective will and the universal will are not grasped as moments of the same totality, even though they show themselves to be bound up with each other, whereas the idea of moral autonomy demands that we grasp the subjective will as being identical with the universal will, in the sense that the determinations of the latter can be understood as expressions of the individual's own rational will. Consequently, if we remain at the level of civil society, individuals must be thought to experience the universal will as something alien to their own wills, with the laws and institutions of the state being viewed merely as limitations on their arbitrary wills, albeit necessary and legitimate ones in so far as they enable these same individuals to pursue their private ends more effectively and serve to protect their own persons and property. This in turn suggests heteronomy of the will, which occurs when the subjective will is determined by something that remains external to it.

From what has been said above, it is evident that Hegel's criticisms of social contract theory are largely motivated by the idea that it turns the relation of the subjective will to the universal will into a merely external one and thus fails to show how the principle of moral autonomy is to be incorporated into the modern state. Although Fichte's contract theory of the state implies such an external relation because right is conceived purely in terms of a limitation on human freedom, albeit a necessary and legitimate one, there is an important sense in which social contract theory implies an act of self-legislation and consequently the idea that the limitations to which one is subject are expressions of one's own will. This is especially true of Kant's contract theory of the state when he describes the conditions that need to be met in order for the particular laws of the state to count as legitimate ones.

Kant does not speak of the social contract as an historical fact but instead regards it as a regulative principle or idea of reason, which can be used to judge the adequacy of individual laws by asking whether such laws could have issued from the united will of a whole nation (TP 297/79). In spite of this element of innovation, Kant's account of the social contract is heavily influenced by Rousseau's version of it. Rousseau claims that the social contract provides the solution to the problem as to how each person, while renouncing his natural freedom, nevertheless obeys only himself and thus remains as free as before. The social contract solves this problem by giving rise to a condition in which all become equal in virtue of the fact that each person, without exception, renounces his natural freedom, so that no one has any interest in making the condition into which he enters burdensome for others, that is to say, one in which there exist unequal rather than mutual relations of dependence.[11] This leads Rousseau to characterize the condition in question as one that is determined by a common interest, which requires each person to submit to the same conditions that he imposes on others.[12] In this respect, the laws that an individual obeys are laws that he himself may reasonably have made, in the sense that they do not put him at a disadvantage in relation to others but do serve to secure his own life and property.

In a similar fashion, Kant states that a human being in a condition of right 'has relinquished entirely his wild, lawless freedom in order to find his freedom as such undiminished, in a dependence upon laws, that is, in a rightful [*rechtlichen*] condition, since this dependence arises from his own lawgiving will' (MS 316). Kant also thinks that he has discovered a principle that can be employed to decide which particular laws could arise from the individual's own will in the sense of being laws to which he could reasonably submit himself. As with the categorical imperative, the principle in question demands that the laws in question do not result in a contradiction (TP 299/80–81). This requirement is designed to guarantee that 'each decides the same thing for all and all for each', so that only 'the general united will of the people' legislates the laws of the state (MS 314). This is simply a restatement of Rousseau's demand that each person submit himself to the same conditions that he imposes on others and one of its main implications, namely, that each individual therefore wills what is common to himself and others rather than willing a particular end that others may not share.

It thus appears that, for Kant, the legitimacy of the various laws of the civil constitution derives from an act of self-legislation, in the sense that people are subject to laws to which they could reasonably have been expected to submit themselves, so that the laws in question can be seen as products of their own rational wills. Each member of the civil constitution thus legislates its own laws, which are therefore just as much expressions of human freedom as limitations on one aspect of it, namely, freedom of choice.[13] Hegel appears to recognize the existence of this element of self-legislation in Kant's theory of right, for he states that Kant's definition of right contains not only the negative determination of a limitation on the arbitrary will, but also the positive element of 'the universal law or so-called "law of reason", which, in line with his characterization of the categorical imperative, amounts to the law of non-contradiction (PR §29A). Although the limitations that right imposes on freedom of choice can in this way be understood as self-imposed ones, so that, as with the concept of moral autonomy, the laws to which individuals are subject are equally the product of their own wills, the fact remains that Kant, like Fichte, stresses the negative conception of right as a limitation on freedom of choice at the expense of the more positive one mentioned above.

This is evident from Kant's thoughts concerning the kind of laws which could have arisen from the individual's own rational will, in the sense of being laws to which he could reasonably have been expected to submit himself. In order to determine the kind of laws which could have arisen from the individual's own rational will, Kant is required to introduce certain principles which are assumed to be valid from his moral theory. One such principle is to be found in Kant's definition of freedom as the freedom of every member of society as a human being (TP 290/74). For Kant clearly here has in mind the idea of moral personality, and hence the concept of the person, which he defines as a subject whose actions can be imputed to him, while nothing can be imputed to a thing because it is the object of a person's free choice which itself lacks freedom (MS 223). Kant further explains what he means by this distinction between persons and things when he points out that although I can be constrained by another to perform actions that serve as the means to his own ends, I can never be constrained by others to have an end (MS 381). In other words, while another human being may employ some form of physical or psychological coercion to compel me to perform an action which serves as the means to one or more of his own ends, this does not imply that I must identify myself with the end in question. On the contrary, if I cannot identify myself with it, I have the capacity to refuse to act as the means to this end, even if it involves risking my own life or livelihood. In the case of a thing, by contrast, it makes no sense to claim that it has the ability to identify or renounce the end towards which it serves as the means, since it lacks the capacity to form ends altogether.

On the basis of the distinction which he makes between persons and things, Kant accords the former an intrinsic value and describes them as ends in themselves, which ought never to be treated merely as means to an end, whereas things are said to possess only a relative value, which allows them to be treated merely as a means to an end (G 428). It is in virtue of their having the status of ends in themselves that persons have certain rights, such as the right not to suffer physical harm at the hands of others or to be unjustly coerced into performing actions. The objection might be made, however, that the capacity of persons to set themselves ends does not by itself suggest that we should accord them the status of ends in themselves, if this is taken to imply that human beings possess a dignity which things lack. After all, the ends which persons set themselves can be of such a kind that one may well wish that they lacked this capacity altogether. However, in order to understand why Kant thinks that human beings possess such dignity, we need to bear in mind the distinction that he makes between subjective ends, which may be motivated by self-interest or merely by physical impulse, and objective (i.e. moral) ends, which are valid for all rational beings (G 427). It is the capacity to adopt objective ends or duties, rather than the capacity to adopt ends in general, which is the source of a human being's dignity. Kant therefore identifies moral personality with the freedom of a rational being under moral laws, and thus distinguishes it from psychological personality, which is merely the capacity for being conscious of one's identity through the different conditions of one's existence (MS 223). In other words, although the general capacity to set themselves ends is enough to distinguish persons from things, persons deserve the status of ends in themselves only in virtue of their having the more specific capacity of being able to set themselves objective ends.

Kant's view of persons as ends in themselves provides the moral foundations of the condition of right guaranteed by the civil constitution by means of coercive laws; for the civil constitution serves to protect the rights which derive from one's having the status of a person.[14] The condition of right therefore comprises various laws that serve to preserve each person's status as an end in himself by protecting his person from physical harm, by allowing him to pursue his own ends in so far as this is compatible with the rights of others to do the same, and by securing any legitimate expressions of his capacity to adopt one content rather than another as the object of his will, such as any legitimately acquired items of property that he may own. The principle of personality thus determines the particular laws of the state by providing a constraint on the kind of laws that could be held to issue from the united general will of the people without contradiction. It would, for example, be contradictory to pass a law that would allow certain persons to be deprived of their status as persons through treating them merely as means to an end instead of free beings, or to pass any laws that infringed the rights which dervive from the principle of personality. In this respect, the laws of the civil constitution are primarily concerned with telling individuals what they are forbidden to do in relation to others.

The laws of the state can therefore be seen as having the primary function of limiting each person's freedom of choice in relation to others so as to guarantee each and every human being the status of a person, as when the law forbids a person to coerce others into acting as the means to the realization of his own personal ends, or when it forbids a person from making someone else's property into the object of his freedom of choice. Kant's theory of right in this respect accords with Fichte's account of right as that which protects persons and their property by means of coercive force.

Although Hegel is critical of this conception of right for understanding the latter almost exclusively in terms of a limitation on freedom of choice, with the result that the relation of the subjective will to the universal will is turned into a merely external one, he nevertheless views it as a constitutive feature of modern ethical life. Indeed, Hegel himself gives expression to the idea that persons are not to be treated as though they were things when he claims that in Roman law no definition of a human being would be possible because the slave could not be subsumed under it. Hegel makes this claim in connection with the idea that the more incoherent and internally contradictory the determinations of a system of right are, the less possible it will be to make definitions within it; for definitions should contain universal determinations, whereas in Roman law the status of the slave, which in Kantian terms is that of means to an end, makes the definition of a human being impossible (PR §2A). In other words, in the case of the slave we would have an individual who belongs to the general type 'human being', but who cannot be subsumed under the definition given in law of this general type. Roman law fails, in short, to recognize the universal which first makes a human being a human being, whereas for Hegel:

> ... if we consider Caius, Titus, Sempronious, together with all the other inhabitants of a city or a country, the fact that they are all human beings [*Menschen*] is not something that they simply have in common; on the contrary, it is what is *universal* in them, it is their *kind*, and none of them would be what he is at all without this kind (EL §175Z).[15]

For Hegel, the universal is the ground or substance of the individual; and the universal is here the concept human being, which is logically prior to any of the contingent features which happen to characterize individual human beings, such as, in the case of the slave, the fact that he is a barbarian, or was captured in battle and sold into slavery, or was the offspring of someone to whom this happened in the past. In short, there is no rational basis for according the slave a different status to the one possessed by his master or the Roman citizen in general, since they are all of the same general type; and this is why the slave represents a contradictory element within Roman law.[16] Hegel, like Kant, can therefore be seen to hold the view that universalizability is a necessary condition of rational law.

Although Hegel clearly accepts Kant's views concerning the kind of laws to which all individuals may reasonably offer their consent, the laws in question, which require an authority equipped with coercive force, have the primary function of setting limits to freedom of choice; and in this respect the conception of right thus arrived at fails to explain the unity of the subjective will and the universal will which for Hegel is constitutive of ethical life. These laws can admittedly be understood as products of the united general will of the people and thus as expressions of human freedom as well as limitations on it. In the next chapter I shall nevertheless argue that a significant difference between Hegel's conception of right and the one to be found in the contract theories of the state offered by Kant and Fichte is that Hegel is better able to emphasize the positive (i.e. self-legislating) aspect of right. He is able to do this, moreover, by rejecting the idea of a general will as it is presented in social contract theory, that is, as a united or general will which is constituted through the composition of many individual wills. We shall see, in fact, that Hegel reinterprets the idea of a general will so as to give an alternative explanation of how individuals are, in principle, able to understand right as an expression of their own wills, so that subjective will and the universal will can be understood as standing in an essential relation to each other.

Before going on to look at Hegel's reinterpretation of the idea of a general will, I shall first describe another important way in which he seeks to subordinate the subjective will to the universal will in a way that does not turn their relation to each other into a merely external one. As is fitting for a theory which has Kant's idea of moral autonomy as one of its main sources of inspiration, Hegel claims that it is through performing their various duties that individuals bring about the identity of their own subjective wills with the universal will, so that the latter is in this sense produced by the individuals whose actions it at the same time determines. Hegel's account of how this happens will lead me to consider the issue of the role of conscience in his theory of modern ethical life and to reintroduce a right which derives from the principle of subjective freedom that I have yet to discuss in relation to Hegel's theory of modern ethical life: the right of the subjective will to have an insight into what it holds to be good or true. In connection with this right, we shall see in the next chapter that although Hegel offers an account of the relation of the subjective will to the universal will which can be explained in terms of the 'external' state or state of necessity, he also attempts to fully establish their essential relation to each other by reinterpreting the idea of a general will.

Duty as the Unity of the Subjective Will and the Universal Will

An important way in which the unity of the subjective will and the universal will is established in ethical life concerns the role that individuals have to play in actualizing the various determinations of the latter. Hegel alludes to this role when he states that the state possesses its actuality 'in the particular *self-consciousness* when this has been raised to its universality' (PR §258). Since, as we shall see, the role played by the subjective will in actualizing the universal will embodied in the various determinations of ethical life is linked to the concept of duty, this role can be seen as forming part of Hegel's attempt to explain the possibility of an ethics which is not alien to the subjective will. Although Hegel accepts the validity of two essential features of the moral standpoint, the idea of moral autonomy and the idea that the individual stands in a relation of 'unqualified obligation' to the good (PR §133), we saw that the moral standpoint by itself in his view fails to provide a set of determinate duties and that this failure is to be remedied by his theory of ethical life. We therefore need to look at Hegel's account of the relation of the various determinations of modern ethical life to the subjective will of the individual so as to gain a better idea of his conception of duty.

Since a later stage of right is held by Hegel to be more concrete than the one that precedes it (PR §30), we must assume that the final stage of right, the state, is more concrete than the earlier stages of right in the sense that it contains the other determinations of right, including the modern family and the laws and institutions of civil society, within itself. Hegel describes the family and the institutions of civil society as together forming the constitution in 'the realm of *particularity*' (PR §265). It is evident that Hegel describes the institutions of civil society in this way because they realize the right of subjective freedom, which demands the satisfaction of the individual's particularity, whether in the form of welfare or in the form of the right to exercise free choice. Hegel also terms the institutions of civil society the legal constitution

(*Rechtsverfassung*) because civil society is made up of institutions whose main function is to protect the lives, property and personal freedom of its members, whereas he terms the set of institutions that make up the political state the constitution of the state (*Staatsverfassung*) (PR §157). This shows that Hegel employs both a narrow and a broader conception of the state; for while the latter consists of the determinations of modern ethical life taken together as a whole, the former is restricted to the political state taken in isolation from the earlier stages of modern ethical life.

The state in the broader sense of the term, that is, the state understood as a politically unified whole, also incorporates the stages of abstract right and morality within itself because it contains institutions, especially those of civil society, whose function is to realize the commandment of universal right and the idea of the welfare of all, while the legal system recognizes the right of knowledge, since individuals are held to be responsible only for what they intended and for consequences that they might have reasonably foreseen as resulting from their actions. In the next section, I shall argue that Hegel's theory of modern ethical life also allows some room for acting in accordance with the demands of one's own conscience.

It is the laws and institutions of the state in the broader sense of the term that in Hegel's view provide ethics with an objective content (PR §144). Hegel's conception of duty therefore concerns the individual's relation to the determinations of the state and the various norms which derive from this relation;[17] and he consequently describes the specific form of virtue that he calls rectitude (*Rechtschaffenheit*) as 'the simple adequacy of the individual to the duties of the circumstances [*Verhältnisse*] to which he belongs' (PR §150). Hegel distinguishes rectitude from virtue as such, which concerns an individual's character, when he claims that an individual's character had a more prominent role to play in ancient ethical life than in its modern counterpart because the laws and institutions of this earlier form of ethical life were in some way deficient, so that this deficiency had to be remedied by 'the distinctive genius of individuals' (PR §150A). In a modern state, by contrast, as long as it has adequate laws and institutions, such a natural conception of virtue would be out of place; for instead of involving the desire to emulate certain extraordinary individuals, modern virtue presupposes the existence of universally valid laws and institutions to which one must simply learn to conform. This is why Hegel claims that the age of the actual virtues is past, whereas the age in which we live is more the age of rectitude (VRP 2 125), which involves acting in a universal manner and not wanting to distinguish oneself from others (VRP 4 404).

This suggests that Hegel holds the view that acting ethically is a rather minor achievement in a state with good laws and institutions. He claims, in fact, that an individual's duties in an ethical community are easy to state because the individual 'must simply do what is prescribed, expressly stated, and known to him within his situation [*in seinen Verhältnisse*]' (PR §150A). In this respect, Hegel's solution to the problem of how we are to identify what is the ethically right thing to do can be compared to Plato's view that the question of moral rectitude cannot be separated from the question concerning the nature of the just *polis*.[18] I shall, however, argue that there are good reasons for rejecting the idea that Hegel thereby reduces the relation of the subjective will to the universal will to one of mere conformity.

Although Hegel considers the laws and institutions of modern ethical life to be universally valid ethical determinations, he recognizes that there is an important sense in which these laws and institutions depend on the same individuals whose duty is to act in conformity with them. For it is only through the conscious activity of these same individuals that the laws and institutions of the state become actual, so that one can think of the universal will embodied in the determinations of ethical life as being a product of the subjective will, which thus brings about its own unity with the universal will. Hegel refers to this feature of ethical life when he claims that the state has 'its mediate existence in the *self-consciousness* of the individual, in the individual's knowledge and activity' (PR §257).

The idea that individuals produce the ethical substance which at the same time determines their thoughts and actions is also to be found in Hegel's account of ethical life in the *Phenomenology of Spirit*. Hegel here claims that although substance, as the universal essence and end, stands over against the individualized reality (i.e. the individual agent), self-consciousness both raises the individualized reality to the level of substance and brings substance down to the level of the individualized reality by acting ethically; so that the end (i.e. the ethical substance), which at first existed only in thought, becomes actual, while self-consciousness produces the unity of itself and substance as its own work and as something that exists (PhG 327–28/444). In other words, the determinations of the ethical substance (i.e. the laws and institutions of the state), which orientate the thoughts and actions of its individual members, are equally the product of its members' theoretical and practical activity.

Although individuals, by acting ethically, produce the ethical substance which determines their thoughts and actions, it should be pointed out that the description of this reciprocal relation between the ethical substance and its members given in the *Phenomenology of Spirit* relates to the ethical life of ancient Greece. This essential feature of ethical life does not therefore tell us anything specific to modern ethical life, which is the subject of Hegel's philosophy of right, whereas the way in which Hegel associates modern ethical life with the principle of subjective freedom implies that modern ethical life is essentially different from the ethical life of the *polis*. There is, for example, the link that Hegel makes between modern ethical life and the idea of the true conscience on the grounds that conscience, which expresses the subject's right to know what right and duty are and to recognize only what it knows to be good and true, is a constitutive feature of the modern world. According to Hegel, the ancient Greek, by contrast, had no conscience, because, 'Right and duty were defined by the law of the state, and no reflection occurred regarding whether they were indeed right and duty' (VG 263/213).[19] We may therefore assume that there is something distinctive about the way in which the unity of the subjective will and the universal will is established in modern ethical life. In the next section and in the next chapter, I intend to show that the distinctive way in which this unity is established in modern ethical life relates to the role that conscience plays in the modern world, both in the shape of the formal conscience and in the shape of the right of the subjective will to recognize nothing as good or true that it does not perceive as rational.

The role that the formal conscience might be thought to play in Hegel's theory of modern ethical life relates to his claim that the latter remedies the moral standpoint's failure to give rise to a set of determinate duties. One reason for this failure can be seen to relate to the great emphasis that the moral standpoint places on inner determinations of the will, such as an agent's good intentions or a feeling of absolute certainty and conviction concerning duty; for this emphasis on what is inner invites the kind of indecision and excessive scrupulousness that Hegel describes in the following passage along with the way in which his theory of ethical life provides the remedy:

> For the person who has turned inwards [*der in sich reflectirte Mensch*] dwells ceaselessly on the matter, broods inwardly, without any powerful feeling of self, without spiritual health. The simple duty therefore liberates him from this malady and brooding. For in doing his duty a person acts in a universally valid manner, and relinquishes his particularity. To be something particular is the malady of reflection. This is moral unhealthiness, [which is] partly a state of dejection, partly self-satisfaction, in which a person is not actual because he is not in harmony with what is objective (VRP 3 491).

We must assume that the duties that liberate the individual from this malady arise from his relation to the various determinations of modern ethical life, so that these determinations can be held to tell this individual how he ought to lead his life. Although this idea goes some way towards undermining the view of Hegel's system as an abstract edifice which provides individuals with no guidance whatsoever as to how they ought to lead their lives, the question remains as to whether Hegel's theory of duty can be said to provide individuals with sufficient guidance as to how they ought to act.

This brings me to a problem that relates to the role played by conscience in the modern world. I argued in the last chapter that Hegel's theory of modern ethical life should in part be viewed as an attempt to solve the problem of ethical subjectivism posed by the formal conscience, which has its roots in Kant's theory of moral judgment. In connection with this problem, I also argued that the role assigned to conscience by both Kant and Fichte appears to raise the possibility of individuals arriving at opposed, but equally well grounded, moral duties, thus leading to what can be described as a collision of duties. In what follows, I intend to argue that Hegel's theory of duty does not rule out the possibility of a collision of duties, and that, given the significance which Hegel attaches to subjectivity in the modern world, of which conscience is a constitutive feature, one could conceive of situations in which this collision of duties occurs within the same person. This collision occurs, moreover, because the laws and institutions of modern ethical life fail to provide the person in question with sufficient guidance as to how to act in the particular situation in which he finds himself.

A Collision of Duties

In his account of ethical life in the *Phenomenology of Spirit*, Hegel mentions two examples of what he considers to be a spurious collision of duties: the 'sorry spectacle' of a collision between passion and duty, and the 'comic' one of a collision between duty and duty (PhG 342–43/465). The first type of collision is not a genuine collision of duties because passion, which is based on the contingency and particularity of feeling, is not on a par with duty, which commands what is universally valid, so that there is, in effect, no real question regarding which side is right. In the case of the second type of collision, passion is mistakenly represented as duty, and in this respect the collision of duties is of essentially the same kind as the first type of collision. Hegel may here be understood to have in mind the fact that a feeling of personal conviction can form the basis of our judgments concerning duty, and the way in which such duties based on personal conviction alone may come into conflict with duties that arise from the individual's relation to the laws and institutions of ethical life. Hegel appears to dismiss this second type of collision rather too quickly, however, for I shall later argue that he thereby masks the important issue of the extent to which his theory of modern ethical life provides individuals with sufficient guidance as to how they should act in particular circumstances.

Hegel nevertheless allows for the possibility of a genuine collision of duties in the case of ancient Greek ethical life, which for him is characterized by a lack of reflective thought. I shall now give a brief account of how this collision of duties comes about and then compare it to certain features of Hegel's theory of modern ethical life. This will lead me to raise the question as to whether or not modern ethical life could give rise to a collision of duties, even though it is alleged to provide conscience with a set of determinate duties.

Hegel's account of the ethical life of ancient Greece in the *Phenomenology of Spirit* is based on Sophocles' play *Antigone.* This should come as no surprise, since, according to Hegel, it is in the works of people such as Sophocles, Aristophanes, Thucydides and Plato that we find the historical expression of what Greek life actually was (VG 177/146). In Sophocles' play, Antigone, daughter of Oedipus, the former ruler of Thebes, comes into conflict with Creon, her uncle, who now rules the city. The conflict in question arises in connection with Creon's edict forbidding anyone to bury the corpse of Antigone's brother, Polyneices, who died attacking the city in an attempt to seize power from his brother, Eteocles. Antigone disobeys Creon's edict and buries Polyneices, whereupon Creon punishes this transgression of his edict by having Antigone imprisoned in a tomb, in which she eventually dies. By refusing to revoke his edict, Creon ends up violating the traditions concerning the burial of the dead associated with the divine powers that are believed to sustain ancient Greek ethical life, thereby bringing ruin upon himself and his family and the city. In Hegel's account of ancient Greek ethical life, the conflict between Antigone and Creon is generalized to become a conflict between the divine law and the human law, with the latter being identified with the male and the former with the female family member. We now need to determine the precise sense in which this conflict between the human law and the divine law involves a genuine collision of duties.

Sophocles' play suggests that the conflict in question involves a genuine collision of ethical duties because Antigone and Creon both make claims that would be viewed as legitimate ones within the *polis*. Antigone, on the one hand, justifies her refusal to obey Creon's edict by appealing to the 'great unwritten, unshakeable traditions', which appear to have existed from time immemorial,[20] whereas human laws change with time, and do not, therefore, appear to possess the same validity as that which tradition prescribes. Creon, on the other hand, appeals to the absolute need for people to obey human laws and those individuals invested with political authority, so as to prevent a condition of anarchy from breaking out, which for a city is the worst of all evils; and it should be noted that in the play itself the force of Creon's argument is immediately acknowledged by the leader of the chorus.[21]

Hegel's account of the conflict between the divine law and the human law accords with the conflict between Antigone and Creon as described in the play itself because he identifies the divine law with an inner essence, the Penates, that is to say, the gods of the hearth, while he identifies the human law with publicly known laws and the government (PhG 329–30/448–49). As we shall see, Hegel's account of the conflict between the divine law and the human law suggests that this conflict involves a genuine collision of duties. Yet Hegel claims that the opposition between the divine law and the human law 'appears as an *unfortunate* collision of duty merely with a reality which possesses no rights of its own' (PhG 343/466); and he also describes the opposition between the two sides of the ethical substance as a superficial one (PhG 329/446). I shall now attempt to explain why Hegel must nevertheless be thought to hold the view that the conflict between the divine law and the human law as it occurs in ancient Greek ethical life involves a genuine collision of ethical duties, in the sense that the agents involved are not in a position to reflect on the one-sidedness of the standpoints that they have come to adopt.

We already know that prior to the appearance of the Sophists and Socrates, reflective thought was not a feature of ancient Greek ethical life; and judging from Sophocles' play, this lack of reflection is typical of the ethical consciousness in so far as it identifies itself with one of the two main ethical powers (i.e. the divine law or the human law) to the exclusion of the other one, which it regards as being less essential than the ethical power with which it identifies itself. Hegel stresses the unreflective nature of the agent's identification with one of the ethical powers to the exclusion of the other when he claims that the ethical consciousness is 'the simple, pure direction of activity towards what is ethically essential, or duty; there is in it no freedom of choice [*Willkür*], and likewise no struggle or indecision' (PhG 342/465).[22] This lack of reflection means that the ethical consciousness is incapable of asking itself whether the claims made in support of the other ethical power might not, after all, be as equally well grounded as the claims that it makes in support of the ethical power with which it identifies itself.

Hegel refers on a number of occasions to the interdependence that characterizes the relation of the human law to the divine law. He claims, for example, that the law which is manifest to the ethical consciousness, whether it be the human law or the divine law, is essentially tied to its opposite, so that the essence of these laws is their unity, even though the ethical consciousness itself carries out one law in opposition to the other one (PhG 347/469). Each ethical power is therefore said to have no advantage over the other that would make it into a more essential moment of the ethical substance (PhG 349/472). I shall now attempt to offer an interpretation of what Hegel means by this interdependence of the divine law and the human law.

One of the main functions performed by the family in ancient Greek ethical life concerns the upbringing of children; and the upbringing of the male members of the family has as its ultimate end a sphere of activity which lies outside the institution of the family, namely, political life, in which the end of the individual's activity becomes the ethical community as a whole, in whose service the male citizen must act in order to prove that he is virtuous (PhG 331/451). The community as a whole is, moreover, the power over all the individual aspects of ancient Greek ethical life, including the various families of which it is made up, since, through its laws and the government which directs its activities, the community prevents any single aspect (e.g. any particular family) from isolating itself from the social whole and acting contrary to the common interest (PhG 334–35/455). In this respect, the human law appears to have priority over the divine law, which Hegel associates with the family.

The family performs another function within ancient Greek ethical life, however: the role of performing the burial rites that tradition prescribes in the event of the death of one of its members. This function takes on a special significance in the case of a male family member who has died performing the highest duty that he has as a citizen, which is to risk his life in the community's struggles against other communities. For in performing the prescribed funeral rites, the sister, to whom this task is entrusted, acts in accordance with the commands of the gods and thus in a way designed to appease the chthonic powers that are held to lend strength to the community in its struggles against other communities. In this respect, the activity of the female member of the family (i.e. the sister) and the activity of the male member of the family (i.e. the brother), which is directed towards the defence of the city, come to have the same object: the preservation of the community as a whole. The family thus helps to preserve the community not only by raising its male members to become virtuous citizens, but also by performing the rites upon which the favour bestowed by the divine powers on the ethical community is believed to depend. In short, a reciprocal relationship exists between the divine law, as represented by the institution of the family, and the human law, as represented by the government and those individuals invested with political authority. Consequently, the unity of ancient Greek ethical life must be thought to depend on the harmony of the human law and the divine law.

I have offered an interpretation which makes sense of a number of things that Hegel has to say about ancient Greek ethical life,[23] including the idea that it appears to exhibit an order and harmony of the ethical powers until it is disturbed by the actions of the two ethical consciousnesses, each of which identifies itself exclusively with one of the ethical powers to the exclusion of the other ethical power (PhG 342/464). The fact that both the divine law and the human law are essential moments of Greek ethical life means, moreover, that each ethical consciousness must be thought to act in accordance with duty, albeit in a wholly unreflective and one-sided manner. When Hegel says that the collision of duties which occurs in ancient Greek ethical life is a superficial one, he cannot, therefore, be seen as claiming that this collision of duties is a spurious one, as is the case with the collision between passion and duty and the comical collision between duty and duty, in which one of the duties is not really a duty. The problem is, instead, that in identifying itself so unreservedly with one of the ethical powers to the exclusion of the other one, the unreflective ethical consciousness shows itself to be blind to the true nature of ancient Greek ethical life as a whole, of which both the human law and the divine law are essential moments.

Since, as previously mentioned, Hegel claims that ancient Greek ethical life only appears to exhibit a harmony of the ethical powers, we must assume that the unity of the ethical powers found in ancient Greek ethical life is an essentially inadequate one, so that the dissolution of this form of ethical life is not simply a result of the way in which the unreflective ethical consciousness comes to identify itself exclusively with one ethical power in opposition to the other one. The conflict which arises between the divine law and the human law should in fact be viewed as a symptom of the inherent limitations of this unity of the ethical powers. With this point in mind, I now intend to compare Hegel's characterization of ancient Greek ethical life with certain features of his theory of modern ethical life, in which one would expect the limitations to which ancient

Greek ethical life is subject to have been overcome. I shall do this by looking at the relation between the divine law and the human law that we find in Hegel's theory of modern ethical life and the role that the ethical consciousness plays in the latter. In connection with the second issue, I shall be led to say more about the role of conscience in modern ethical life and to suggest that Hegel must concede that a genuine collision of duties could occur in the latter.

A major difference between the ancient and modern forms of ethical life is that Hegel makes the human law largely independent of the divine law, which is no longer identified with the particular institution of the family, whereas this institution forms the link between the human law and the divine law in ancient Greek ethical life. The independence of the human law of the divine law in modern ethical life finds expression in the separation of Church and state which, according to Hegel, has brought about a division which benefits both the Church and thought in so far as their rationality and freedom are concerned (PR §270A). Hegel's main reasons for making this claim are easy to identify in the light of his recognition of the principle of subjective freedom, which for him marks a decisive break between the ancient and the modern world.

To begin with, to base the state on religion would ultimately mean basing it on an authority which, itself based on religious texts or traditions that have been handed down from generation to generation, is merely given, and as such conflicts with the right of the subject to have insight into what it holds to be good or true. This issue is admittedly made more complicated by the fact that Hegel claims to have demonstrated the rationality of the Christian religion in his philosophy of religion. Nevertheless, to base the state on religion would still conflict with an individual's right to experience the satisfaction of his particularity and his right to identify with the objects of his concern if any individual were forced to acknowledge a particular historical religion as the basis of the state's authority over him, even though he himself lacked any inner conviction of its truth and divinity.

The claim that the division between state and Church equally benefits the latter might therefore be understood as meaning that any attempt to coerce individuals into holding certain religious beliefs to be true and to base all secular authority on these beliefs would be contrary to true religion, which itself demands an inner conviction concerning the truth and divinity of its doctrines. Any attempt to force individuals into recognizing its authority would, in short, be a sign of corruption and weakness rather than a sign of religious truth. Consequently, although Hegel thinks that the religious disposition can reinforce the ethical one, he restricts himself to making the demand that the state ought to require all its citizens to belong to a religious community, though to any one they please, since the state can have no say in the content of religious belief in so far as it relates to the subject's inwardness (PR §270A). Yet even in making this lesser demand, Hegel goes against his own recognition of the right of subjective freedom, which clearly requires that an individual should not be compelled to belong to a religious community if he does not experience an inner conviction of the truth of any religion whatsoever.

The independence of modern ethical life of religious authority implies that the preservation of the social whole can no longer be thought to depend on the family's performance of certain religious rites that are demanded and sanctioned by divine law. The institution of the modern family therefore falls firmly under the domain of the human law in modern ethical life, whereas in ancient Greek ethical life this institution served as the link between the human law and the divine law. Consequently, if the conflict between Antigone and Creon were transposed to the arena of modern ethical life, Creon would appear to be in the right in so far as he asserts the validity of the dictum *salus reipublicae suprema lex* in opposition to the demands of religious authority; for any attempt to justify one's disobedience of human laws by appealing to religious tradition and the necessity of keeping the gods on one's side could not be recognized as a valid one in the modern state. Indeed, in his discussion of the relation of religion to the state in the philosophy of right, Hegel himself points out that inward religiosity may result in a fanaticism which threatens the destruction of all ethical relations; and against such religious fanaticism he claims that 'educated humanity has actualized and become conscious of rational existence [*Dasein*], political institutions, and laws' in the course of history (PR §270A).

The claim that educated humanity has actualized and become conscious of political institutions and laws in the course of history suggests two things: the idea that modern ethical life is a more adequate expression of the human law than ancient Greek ethical life ever was; and the idea that humanity has achieved a different, more reflective, type of ethical attitude. These two ideas can be seen to invite the question as to whether or not the developments that have led to a more adequate form of ethical life, such as the emancipation of the state from religion, rule out the possibility of the kind of ethical collision which Hegel thinks led to the disintegration of ancient Greek ethical life. They also invite the question as to whether or not a change in the ethical consciousness itself may prevent a genuine collision of duties from taking place in modern ethical life. In what follows, I shall argue that these two features of modern ethical life, whether taken separately or taken together, do not rule out the possibility of a genuine collision of duties because the laws and institutions of modern ethical life cannot be said to provide individuals with sufficient guidance as to how they are to act in particular circumstances, so that in many cases individuals will themselves have to reflect on what is the right thing to do.

With regard to the question as to whether or not the emergence of a more adequate form of ethical life may prevent a collision of duties, I shall suggest in what follows that the separation of the human law (i.e. the state) from the divine law (i.e. religion) which has taken place in modern ethical life does not preclude the possibility of a collision of duties taking place within the domain of the human law itself, such as a conflict between one's duties as a family member and one's duties as the member of a wider social whole. The type of collision in question no longer needs to be represented as a collision between two individual ethical consciousnesses, however, but may instead, given Hegel's views on subjectivity, be understood to take place within a single ethical consciousness, so that it is perhaps better to speak of a conflict of duties rather than a collision of duties. In this way, I shall also be led to address the issue as to whether or not a change in the character of the ethical consciousness can prevent a genuine collision of duties from taking place in modern ethical life. I first need, however, to say more about the place of the family in modern ethical life and to then indicate a feature of the modern ethical consciousness which, in Hegel's view, distinguishes it from the ancient Greek ethical consciousness.

Although Hegel deprives the modern family of the vital religious role that it plays in ancient Greek ethical life, he still thinks of it as an ethical totality in which one is present not as an independent person but as a member (PR §158). Moreover, in relation to its function of bringing up children, the modern family, like its counterpart in the ancient world, has as its ultimate end a sphere of activity which lies beyond it; for it prepares its members for participation in society as a whole, even though the capacities and dispositions which the modern family nurtures in the child may differ from those which earlier forms of the family sought to nurture. As the most basic social unit and as an institution which performs the vital role of preparing its younger members for participation in the other institutions of modern ethical life, the family is as essential to the latter as it was to ancient Greek ethical life. The fact that the family is an essential moment of modern ethical life invites the question as to whether or not it could give rise to duties that conflict with the duties that arise in connection with the other essential determinations of modern ethical life, thus producing a collision of duties. Before answering this question, we first need to turn to a change in the modern ethical consciousness which distinguishes it from the type of ethical consciousness found in ancient Greek ethical life.

While the ethical consciousness found in ancient Greek ethical life was an unreflective one until the time of the Sophists and Socrates, we have seen that Hegel accords both the Sophists and Socrates an historical significance that derives from the way in which they helped to introduce the demand for insight into what one holds to be good or true. His claim that educated humanity has become conscious of political institutions and laws in the course of history can therefore be interpreted as meaning that humanity has gained greater insight into the rationality of these laws and institutions, or has at least become capable of gaining such insight into them, with this potential insight stemming from changes that have taken place with regard to the character of these laws and institutions. The reflective thought that distinguishes the modern ethical consciousness from its counterpart in the ancient world can, however, be seen to have another implication which this time concerns Hegel's recognition of the fact that the various determinations of ethical life can become actual only through the conscious activity of individuals. Although this is true of both the ancient and the modern forms of ethical life, I now intend to argue that Hegel's views on the reflective nature of the modern self imply a significant difference between the way in which modern individuals may perform their social roles and the way in which their counterparts in the ancient Greek world performed them. The difference in question relates to the fact that the performance of a social role will in many cases involve more than a merely mechanical process in which individuals simply act in accordance with pre-established rules and procedures, with the rule or procedure determining everything that needs to be done. The question thus arises as to how individuals decide what to do in situations in which sufficient guidance as to how they are to act is lacking; and I shall argue that, for Hegel, there is something distinctive about the way in which modern individuals tend to make final decisions in such cases of ethical indeterminacy.

In one of his lectures on the philosophy of right, Hegel claims that in certain situations it must simply be left up to the individual to decide what to do in such cases, and that the decisive factor will then be that which we call character, so that to always demand knowledge of what one should do amounts to wanting to be relieved of the effort of having a character (VRP 2 119). This reference to character brings to mind Hegel's account of the ancient Greek ethical consciousness in the *Phenomenology of Spirit*, in which its identification with one of the ethical powers to the exclusion of the other is described as character (PhG 343/466). Since Hegel thinks that reflective thought is a defining feature of the modern world, we might expect, however, that something more than character, which is largely a given fact, has a role to play in deciding what to do when sufficient guidance as to how one is to act is lacking. Moreover, Hegel's account of the role performed by the monarch in modern ethical life points towards a distinctly modern way of deciding what to do in such cases of ethical indeterminacy, while also showing that such indeterminacy is an inescapable feature of modern ethical life.

The monarch's role concerns among other things the need for final decisions to be made regarding affairs of state, decisions that can be made only by an individual human subject (PR §279). Although Hegel thinks that the other parts of the constitution place limits on the powers of the monarch, who must rule in accordance with them (VRP 1 162), he occasionally stresses the arbitrary nature of the monarch's decisions, as when he states that the monarch's final 'I will' is needed to cut short the endless reasons for and against which can be given in relation to all things (PR §279A). Hegel compares this final 'I will' to the way in which priests in the ancient world examined the entrails of animals in order to reach a final decision concerning affairs of state, whereas in the modern world self-consciousness has internalized this element of contingency, which is therefore no longer made to depend on external nature (VRP 1 163).[24] The reason Hegel gives for this change is that human beings in the ancient world 'were not yet strong enough to perceive this decision *within* their own being' (PR §279A). The change is question can therefore be attributed to the increasingly reflective nature of the modern self and the greater self-certainty to which it gives rise, as described by Hegel himself in his accounts of the person and the moral subject.

Although Hegel's account of the role of the monarch suggests that in modern ethical life the need to make a final decision will take the form of an arbitrary decision on the part of the individual for whom specific guidance concerning how he is to act is lacking, one could demand that the individual in question should attempt to reach the right decision by seriously examining the various possibilities open to him and by taking into consideration the views of others, just as, according to Hegel, the monarch should base his decisions on the advice of his ministers (PR §283). In other words, one should seek to work out what is the right thing to do in the particular circumstances by reflecting on the matter in hand, by trying not to let private interest or prejudice alone determine one's judgment, by considering all possibilities and their likely consequences, and by listening to the views of others while not blindly accepting what they have to say. In short, people should attempt to conscientiously think the matter over and seek to arrive at a decision which they are personally convinced is the right one in the circumstances.

The demands mentioned above can be seen as examples of what Kant has in mind when he speaks of conscience, though this time the role of conscience is not to apply a universal rule but to decide what to do in the absence of any clear rule or principle of action. Given his views on the reflective nature of the modern self, I would argue that Hegel must hold that one's own conscience will be the final court of appeal when one's actions cannot be completely determined by any of the ethical norms deriving from one's relation to the laws and institutions of modern ethical life, just as it is for Kant when it comes to applying the categorical imperative to a given maxim. Admittedly, even an ancient Greek may have reflected on what he was to do in situations when clear guidance was lacking to him, in the sense of deliberating on what would be the best thing to do in the circumstances. It could be argued, however, that modern individuals may also consider it to be a moral duty to reflect on what they are to do in the given circumstances and to reach a decision which they are personally convinced is the right one. In any case, the significance which Hegel accords reflective thought in the modern world implies that for him the moral conscience must be considered to be an integral feature of modern ethical life, so that all that can reasonably be demanded of a person in cases of ethical indeterminacy is that he strives to work out in a responsible fashion what is the right thing to do in the circumstances and to act on the basis of his convictions. Therefore, instead of saying that to always demand knowledge of what one should do amounts to wanting to be relieved of the effort of having a character, Hegel should have said that such a demand amounts to wanting to be relieved of the burden of having a conscience. As we shall now see, this understanding of the matter raises the possibility of a genuine collision of duties in modern ethical life, or it might be better to say a conflict of duties, since the example that I shall give concerns a collision of duties that occurs in relation to the same individual's different social roles.

Hegel appears to allow that a genuine collision of duties can take place in modern ethical life when he claims that even within an ethical order whose relations are fully developed and actualized, virtue 'in the proper sense' may have its place when these relations come into collision (PR §150A). Virtue in the proper sense of the term is a matter of character for Hegel, namely, an individual's propensity to act ethically; it is thus a constant feature of a person's character and involves consistently acting in an ethical manner (PR §150, including Z). Although a person's character may certainly have a decisive role to play in cases of ethical indeterminacy, I have already argued that Hegel must also grant that conscience will have a role to play in modern ethical life. I now intend to give a particular example of how, in playing this role, conscience can give rise to a conflict of duties.

If they are going to be genuine duties for Hegel, the duties in question must derive from an individual's relation to the laws and institutions of modern ethical life. The example of a conflict of duties that I shall use therefore concerns an individual's duties as both the member of a family and a member of society as a whole; and it is not difficult, I believe, to conceive of a situation in which one's role as family member comes into conflict with one's role as a member of society. For instance, imagine a situation in which a father has somehow discovered that his son has committed a crime, even though no one else suspects him of having committed it. Although it is not necessary to provide concrete details to make my point, the situation in question should be understood to have the following features: the crime is one that was not committed against any individual person or particular group of individuals (e.g. another family), but was instead committed against a public or private institution (e.g. a company), and is serious enough in the eyes of the law to warrant a custodial sentence, with the son being old enough to have such a sentence passed on him.

It is conceivable that in such a situation the father, who we shall here presume is both a conscientious father and an upright citizen, would experience a conflict of duties: for, on the one hand, he will recognize the need for public laws to be obeyed and the need for individuals who are accused on good grounds of breaking the law to be subjected to an independent judicial process; yet, on the other hand, after having reflected deeply on the matter, he may be convinced that, given the nature of the crime and his knowledge of his son's character, the right thing for him to do would be to deal with the matter himself. In this way, the father experiences a conflict of duties, with his duties as a parent coming into conflict with his duties as a member of society as a whole, and he resolves this conflict according to the dictates of his own conscience. How, then, does such an example fit in to Hegel's theory of modern ethical life?

An obvious response would be to claim that the conflict in question is not a genuine one, since one of the duties is not on a par with the other one. For the father's duty towards his son, which makes him reluctant to inform the authorities of the latter's crime, is subordinate to his duty to respect the publicly known laws of the state, which are not based on the contingency of feeling but instead possess objective validity. It cannot be said, therefore, that the determinations of modern ethical life in this case fail to provide the individual in question with sufficient guidance as to how he is to act. This response is suggested by Hegel himself when he states that one right is subordinate to another, so that ethical duties deriving from a higher sphere of right must be assumed to trump duties deriving from a lower sphere of right (PR §30A). This type of response arguably fails to do justice, however, to what it means to fulfil one's duties as a family member. Rather than interpreting Hegel's position as stating that one social role (e.g. one's role as citizen) gives rise to duties that have priority over those to which another social role (e.g. one's role as parent) gives rise, I intend to argue that a more complex position, which avoids such an either/or view of the matter, can be attributed to him; one that appears to show a greater appreciation of the role that moral conflict can play in our lives. My argument rests on a distinction that can be made regarding the extent to which Hegel's theory of modern ethical life is intended to limit conscience, which, in its merely formal shape, gives rise to the problem of ethical subjectivism.

The extent to which Hegel's philosophy of right aims to counter the ethical subjectivism of the formal conscience can be interpreted in two ways. On the one hand, there is the strong claim that the determinations of modern ethical life provide individuals with sufficient guidance as to how they are to act in all circumstances, so that appeals to conscience alone would neither be necessary nor justifiable in the context of modern ethical life. We cannot, however, attribute this strong claim to Hegel, for, as I have already shown, he accepts that there will be cases in which sufficient guidance as to how one is to act is lacking; and I argued that, given his views on the reflective character of the modern self, we can attribute to him the view that conscience will have an important role to play in determining what an agent decides to do in such cases. On the other hand, there is the weaker claim that the various determinations of ethical life give rise to a set of social norms which provide general guidance but do not, and cannot, completely determine how individuals are to act in all circumstances, so that people will to some extent be justified in appealing to their consciences when seeking to explain their actions to others.

One implication of attributing to Hegel this weaker claim would be that appeals to conscience might be considered to have some legitimacy even when conscience itself appears to generate a conflict of duties in connection with different social roles deriving from one's relation to the laws and institutions of modern ethical life. For it seems unreasonable to maintain that although conscience may have an important role to play in cases of ethical indeterminacy, it can be accorded no legitimacy whatsoever when an individual is confronted by ethical norms which, from the standpoint of the agent in question, appear to generate conflicting requirements. Moreover, if Hegel were to argue that a conflict of duties cannot in fact be said to arise in such cases because some ethical duties, in virtue of their less subjective basis, trump other ethical duties, he would arguably be in danger of making the performance of a social role into a purely mechanical kind of activity; yet this would be at odds with the idea that acting in accordance with duty is to be seen as an expression of autonomy. Therefore, just as Hegel argues that to demand a rule of action for every particular case amounts to wanting to be relieved of the effort of having a character, the demand for a set of ethical norms that completely determine how one is to act in each and every situation could be seen as amounting to the wish to be relieved of the responsibility of having to make difficult moral choices, that is to say, of having a conscience. The making of such choices and accepting responsibility for them is, in short, a vital aspect of what it means to be a moral agent, and this is precisely what Hegel thinks modern individuals are or ought to be.

One way in which modern ethical life can be held to reflect the legitimacy of appeals to conscience can, in fact, be related to the example of the father who is personally convinced that the right thing for him to do is to deal with the matter himself rather than informing the relevant authorities of his son's crime. For he could himself be prosecuted for perverting the course of justice should his son's crime and his knowledge of it ever come to light; yet even if the father were found guilty of this crime, the judge presiding over his trial, if suitably convinced of the father's good intentions and conscientiousness, could take the view that his having acted in accordance with the dictates of his conscience should be seen as a mitigating factor. In this respect, the practice of applying laws to particular violations of them can tell us something important about the attitudes and values underpinning modern ethical life and informing its practices, which in this particular case is the recognition of appeals to conscience. This is similar to the way in which the fact that Oedipus, in spite of his ignorance of the circumstances, was held to be guilty of the crimes of parricide and incest, tells us something significant about this stage of ancient Greek ethical life. Modern ethical life will, in short, reflect the greater value that subjectivity is accorded in the modern world, both in terms of its content, as when particular laws and institutions serve to realize the principle of subjective freedom, and in terms of the attitudes and beliefs of its members. These attitudes and beliefs are also reflected in what are held to be unacceptable grounds for not acting in conformity with the laws of the state; for what might count as a mitigating factor in a different type of society, such as the need to uphold the honour of one's family, is less likely to count as one in modern ethical life, in which such ideas do not have the same role to play as they do in more traditional societies.

As it stands, there is, however, a problem with this interpretation of Hegel's theory of modern ethical life, which appears to concede conscience a greater degree of significance and independence than one might have expected given Hegel's criticisms of the ethical subjectivism of the formal conscience. I have already touched upon this problem, which concerns the fact that both Kant and Fichte, whose accounts of conscience invite the problem of ethical subjectivism, provide theories of right and thus set clear limits to the extent to which appeals to conscience can be held to have any validity in so far as an agent's external actions are concerned. One might therefore ask whether there is really a substantial difference between Hegel's theory of right and the theories of right offered by Kant and Fichte, in spite of the way in which Hegel criticizes social contract theory for turning the relation of the subjective will to the universal will into a merely external one; a type of relation which he thinks is incommensurate with the idea of moral autonomy.

Although I have already described how the unity of the subjective will and the universal will is achieved by individuals producing, through their own conscious activity, the ethical substance which at the same time determines their thoughts and actions, we saw that this is a feature common to the ancient and modern forms of ethical life. I now intend to show that Hegel also explains the unity of the subjective will and the universal will in a specifically modern way by relating it to the principle of subjective freedom and to the right of the subjective will to recognize nothing that it does not perceive as rational. We need to turn to Hegel's account of the different types of ethical attitude that may characterize an individual's relation to the laws and institutions of the modern state so as to discover how he attempts to accommodate this right within his theory of modern ethical life. One important way in which individuals gain insight into the rationality of modern ethical life will be seen to relate to the kind of instrumental attitude which Hegel associates with the 'external' state or state of necessity. We shall see, however, that he identifies a higher form of insight that he thinks demonstrates the unity of the subjective will and the universal will in a way that accords with the idea of moral autonomy, which demands that the ethical norms to which individuals are subject can be understood as an expression of their own wills.

Chapter 4: The Rationality of Modern Ethical Life

The Ethical Attitude

Although Hegel seeks to explain the unity of the subjective will and the universal will in a way that accords with the right of individuals to have insight into the rationality of the various determinations of modern ethical life, he allows that an individual's relation to the ethical substance and its determinations may not involve such insight or, as is more typical of modern ethical life, only a deficient form of it. This deficient form of insight will be seen to relate to the type of instrumental conception of the state which Hegel associates with the 'external' state or state of necessity. He nevertheless considers it to be an integral feature of the modern world and preferable to an absence of insight, which would mean that people experienced their social world as something merely given.

Although Hegel occasionally stresses this element of givenness (PR §146), he does not think that the fact that individuals experience their social world as something given rules out the possibility of demonstrating the rationality of modern ethical life. Indeed, if Hegel held this view of the matter, it would make little sense for him to speak of the right of the subjective will to have insight into what it holds to be good or true; each individual would instead simply have to accept the authority of the existing social order of which he happens to be a member.[1] The only justification that could then be given of this social order would be the brute fact that it exists, or that it was, for example, created by God and forms an object of divine favour. In his philosophy of right, Hegel clearly rules out the idea that the mere fact of its existence is enough to justify the existing social order when he explicitly criticizes two types of state: the patriarchal state, which he criticizes because knowledge is the essential form of spirit, whereas life in this type of state is regulated by feeling and habit or by oracles and divine authority; and the feudal state, in which the whole is held together by various ossified hereditary rights, so that what counts as valid does so only because it was held to be valid in the past (VRP 2 209).

Hegel also speaks of 'the *objective* will' which lacks self-consciousness and is therefore 'immersed in its object or condition', and as examples of this objective will he cites the will of the child, the ethical will, the will of the slave, and the superstitious will (PR §26). The objective will is here to be understood as a will that is subject to an authority which remains alien to it. The child and the slave are subject to an alien authority because they are made to obey another person's will (i.e. the will of the parent and the master), while the superstitious will obeys without understanding why it does so, as when it simply accepts as being true and binding on its own subjective will a priest's interpretation of the commandments of God.[2] The inclusion of the ethical will among these examples of the objective will implies that the ethical consciousness can also be subject to an external authority; and in what follows we shall see that for Hegel the realization of the right of the subjective will to have insight into what it holds to be good or true is the means by which this element of externality is overcome. Consequently, even though he recognizes that some people will not feel a need to have insight into the rationality of the laws and institutions of modern ethical life, Hegel must be thought to hold the view that individuals must in principle be able to attain such insight. In the philosophy of right, Hegel suggests two different ways in which it is possible for individuals to gain insight into the rationality of modern ethical life, with one form of insight being deficient in comparison with the other one. We must now turn to the different types of ethical attitude which Hegel thinks can characterize an individual's relation to his social world and its various determinations so as to identify these two forms of insight.

To begin with, Hegel describes the subject's relation to the ethical substance and its laws and 'powers' as 'immediate and closer to identity than even [a relationship of] *faith* or *trust*' (PR §147). Among the ethical powers, Hegel includes marriage, respect (*Pietät*) and the state; and he claims that these ethical powers govern the lives of individuals and appear indifferent to individuality, so that the individual is only an accident in relation to them (VPR 4 397). The independence that Hegel here accords the ethical powers might be considered to be at odds with the idea that the social world to which individuals belong depends for its very existence on the collective activity of their own wills. Hegel's point is that it would nevertheless be a mistake for any particular individual to think of himself as being anything more than an accident in relation to the social substance because even though in certain cases not just anyone could effectively perform the social role which person *x* performs, since factors such as the possession of a particular skill or talent here come into play, this does not mean that person *x* is completely irreplaceable; the performance of a social role is not, in other words, a matter of genius, in which case no one else but this specific person would be capable of achieving the same result. We can therefore easily imagine other individuals performing particular social roles instead of the individuals who just happen to perform them at any given time. The laws and institutions of ethical life are not, in short, dependent on this or that specific individual for their existence, even though they could not have come into being and could not continue to exist without individuals making them effective. The examples that Hegel gives of the ethical powers show, moreover, that for him ethical life consists not only of laws and institutions, such as marriage and the family, but also of the duties and dispositions that arise in relation to them, such as familial piety and an attitude of respect towards the state itself.

Although Hegel describes the subject's relation to the ethical substance and its laws and powers as an immediate experience of identity, we shall see that the unification of the subjective will and the universal will achieved in modern ethical life is typically far less immediate than this. Hegel already implies a less immediate kind of relation when he speaks of an ethical attitude based on a feeling of faith or trust towards the laws and powers of the ethical substance; a type of relation which must be thought to differ from an immediate identity because faith and trust only arise with the emergence of reflection (PR §147A). In other words, a relation of faith or trust implies the separation of the subject from the object of its faith or trust. This understanding of the individual's relation to the ethical substance and its laws and powers is, of course, in line with Hegel's view that a reflective attitude is a defining feature of the modern self.

This more reflective relation to the ethical substance and its laws and powers is, in fact, what allows Hegel to speak of one's having duties towards them; for the concept of duty presupposes that one stands in a relation to the good (i.e. a relation in which one 'ought' to do one's duty), whereas the standpoint of natural ethical life for Hegel consists in an immediate identity which has yet to be dissolved by reflective thought. This distinction between the immediate identity characteristic of natural forms of ethical life and the more reflective kind of relation found in later forms of the latter leads Hegel to claim that before Socrates came along the Athenians were ethical but not moral, since they did what was rational in the circumstances without reflecting on what they were doing and without knowing that they were excellent human beings; whereas morality also involves the knowledge that this thing, as opposed to that one, is good (VGP I 445/388). In other words, before Socrates the Greeks lacked the ability to reflect on the nature of the laws, institutions, customs and traditions that made up their social world and were therefore not in the position to gain insight into the rationality (or lack of it) of this social world, which they instead encountered as something merely given, like a natural phenomenon whose laws they did not understand. Although this inability to reflect on the nature and content of their social world meant that the Greeks did not themselves experience their social world as being alien to themselves, such dependence on what remains merely given means that the Greeks were not fully free. In a later more reflective age, by contrast, such as the one that in time came to characterize ancient Greek ethical life itself, this lack of insight can result in an experience of alienation in relation to one's social world.[4]

It is not surprising, then, that Hegel should describe the political disposition, or patriotism in general, as one of trust in his philosophy of right (PR §268), thus implying a separation of the subject from the object of its trust and a more reflective attitude towards that which forms the content of one's thoughts and actions. In the same passage in which he describes the political disposition as one of trust, Hegel describes this disposition also as the consciousness that one's own substantial and particular interest is preserved and contained in the interest and end of the state. This reference to the preservation of one's particular interest in the end and interest of the state suggests that the feeling of trust which one has towards the state is in large part mediated by the awareness that one's private interests are inextricably linked with the interests of the state as a whole. This brings me to the third type of ethical attitude that Hegel mentions, which involves an 'insight grounded on reasons [*Einsicht durch Gründe*]' (PR §147A). As we shall see, this type of insight consists in individuals being able to give themselves good reasons for accepting their social roles and for conforming to society's norms, so that it appears to turn the relation of the subjective will to the universal will into a merely external one. This type of insight closely relates, moreover, to Hegel's attempt to accommodate subjective freedom within his theory of modern ethical life.

Hegel clearly thinks that this third type of ethical attitude, which involves an insight based on good reasons, is characteristic of the modern world, in which human beings must enter the 'court' of the reflective understanding and search for reasons [*nach Gründe forschen*] (VRP 3 487). As examples of the kind of reason that he has in mind, Hegel cites particular ends, interests and considerations (PR §147A). This suggests that Hegel is thinking specifically of such reasons as the fact that one is best able to realize one's own personal ends and interests in the state because its various laws and institutions serve to protect the common interest which arises on the basis of the condition of mutual dependence that he calls the system of needs, thus giving individuals a sense of security and well-being. In more general terms, it might be said that individuals recognize that the state provides them with the best chance of maximizing their own happiness, as they conceive of it, together with the happiness of others, especially those people closest to them and the people with whom they must cooperate in order to effectively pursue their own ends and interests. This kind of instrumental reasoning is ultimately based on self-interest, and it is arguably typical of the type of reason that a reasonably successful and contented member of civil society would give himself for accepting his place within society and for acting in conformity with its norms. It can be viewed as a form of insight into the rationality of modern ethical life because instead of resting on an unthinking acceptance of one's social world, it presupposes that individuals have reached the stage at which they have developed a clear understanding of what requirements must be met in order for their social world to qualify as a good one, such as the requirement that the social order should provide individuals with the means of achieving happiness and well-being, or should not, at the very least, prove to be counterproductive in relation to these ends.

Hegel's acceptance of the fact that this type of reasoning has an important role to play in modern ethical life is not surprising given his recognition of the right of the subject to experience the satisfaction of its particularity. It also accords with the importance that he attaches to the institutions of civil society which give rise to a feeling of security and well-being, as when he describes them as 'the firm foundation of the state and of the trust and disposition of individuals towards it' (PR §265). The idea here seems to be that the way in which these institutions serve to accommodate subjective freedom within modern ethical life leads individuals to identify themselves more closely with the interests of the state as a whole, which is recognized to be the ultimate condition of their happiness and well-being. This understanding of the matter helps to explain the following claim that Hegel makes:

> The principle of modern states has enormous strength and depth because it allows the principle of subjectivity to attain fulfilment in the *self-sufficient extreme* of personal particularity, while at the same time *bringing it back to substantial unity* and so preserving this unity in the principle of subjectivity itself (PR §260).

In other words, the unity of the subjective will and the universal will is achieved in modern ethical life through individuals identifying themselves more closely with the modern state and willing its existence on account of the way in which it serves to satisfy their particularity. This leads Hegel to make a firm distinction between modern patriotism and earlier forms of patriotism. He describes modern patriotism as follows:

> Patriotism, the interest the individual has in seeing that his state flourishes and is held in respect, has these two elements: on the one hand, the interest of the individual for the universal as such, and, on the other, the fact that the individual thereby satisfies his own particularity (VRP 4 482).

Hegel thus holds the view that modern individuals identify themselves with the state largely because they recognize that the satisfaction of their particularity is inextricably linked to the preservation and welfare of the state as a whole. This highly mediated relation between the subjective will and the universal will can be usefully compared to the following description of the patriotism which was, according to the young Hegel, typical of an ancient Greek or Roman:

> The idea of his country or of his state was the invisible and higher reality for which he strove, which impelled him to effort; it was the final end of *his* world or in his eyes the final end of *the* world, an end which he found manifested in the realities of his daily life or which he himself co-operated in manifesting and maintaining. Confronted by this idea, his own individuality vanished; it was only this idea's maintenance, life, and persistence that he asked for, and these were things which he himself could make realities. It could never or hardly ever have struck him to ask or beg for persistence or eternal life for his own individuality. Only in moments of inactivity or lethargy could he feel the growing strength of a purely self-regarding wish (PCR 205/154–55).

As compared to this ancient form of patriotism, in which the individual's only interest is the universal as such, modern patriotism, with its added incentive of the satisfaction of one's particularity, appears to be a much weaker form of patriotism. Hegel thinks, however, that once the principle of subjective freedom has entered human consciousness, any attempt to exclude it from the state is bound to result in the particular will asserting itself in other more destructive ways, as when, in the Greek states and the Roman Republic, the appearance of subjectivity led to the overthrow of the existing social order (PR §206A). Hegel consequently does not argue for the complete suppression of the particular will. The latter must instead be accommodated within the state and made to serve a higher end so as to prevent it from becoming a destructive force within the state; and Hegel thinks that the state's ability to do this constitutes its peculiar strength. Hegel must therefore be seen to assign civil society an essential mediating function within his theory of modern ethical life since it is the sphere of the latter in which the subject's particularity finds its satisfaction, thus giving individuals an incentive for acting in conformity with the laws and institutions of modern ethical life and for willing their existence. The subject's particularity does not, however, remain an end in itself within Hegel's theory of modern ethical life; for in serving to strengthen an individual's identification of himself with the state and its interests, the satisfaction of the subject's particularity turns out to be a means of preserving the ethical whole, which forms the true end of ethical life.

Although the mediating function that Hegel thus assigns to civil society allows him to explain how the unity of the subjective will and the universal will is achieved in a distinctly modern way, the unity in question must be considered to be a deficient one in the light of his criticisms of the 'external' state of social contract theory. For the mediating function performed by civil society brings to mind the idea of a common interest which has its ultimate basis in private interest, with the result that the state can be understood simply as the means of realizing this common interest; yet this conception of ethical life is compatible with the external relation between the subjective will and the universal will which Hegel thinks is characteristic of the 'external' state or state of necessity. In this respect, Hegel's theory of modern ethical life allows us to think of the contented *bourgeois* as being someone who identifies himself with the laws and institutions of modern ethical life for purely prudential reasons, and thus remains a *bourgeois* rather than also becoming a *citoyen.* This problem can be further illustrated with reference to the institution of modern ethical life which for Hegel provides the *bourgeois* with his main source of universal activity: the corporation.

The corporation is an institution made up of people who pursue the same trade or occupation, and this is why Hegel describes it as being characteristic of the estate of trade and industry (PR §250). He associates membership of a corporation with the possession of a particular skill (PR §251); it is in fact the corporation which sets the standards that determine whether an individual is skilled or able enough to practise a trade or occupation (PR §§252, 254). In other words, the corporation confers official recognition on an individual's skills, and is therefore to be seen as an important source of self-identity and self-respect, or honour, as Hegel himself calls it (PR §253A). The corporation also seeks to protect the particular and common interests of its members (PR §§252, 255), as when it guarantees their livelihoods (PR §253) and attempts to further the common interest of its members in relation to the political state by electing representatives, who then form part of the legislature (PR §308). This means that the relation of the members of a corporation to the political state is an indirect one based on a common interest, which need not accord with the universal interest which the political state has as its end. Hegel therefore concedes that in modern states the citizens (*Bürger*) have only a limited share in the universal business of the state, with the corporation forming the main source of the universal activity which the modern state does not always offer its citizens (PR §255Z).[5]

Hegel's claim that the corporation forms the main source of universal activity for many people should not be taken to mean that these people consciously make the universal as such (i.e. the ethical whole to which they belong) into the end of their activity. Hegel can admittedly with good reason describe the corporation as constituting the return of the ethical to civil society (PR §249), since, as members of a corporation, individuals become part of a wider social group, thus transcending the atomism which otherwise characterizes civil society; and the role of the corporation can therefore be aptly described as the socialization (*Vergesellschaftlichung*) of the disunited parts of civil society.[6] Yet the end of the corporation remains a 'limited and finite' one (PR §256) because its direct object is the particular and common interests of its members. In other words, the corporation represents an enlightened form of self-interest. Consequently, it is not the case that the *bourgeois* becomes a *citoyen*, that is to say, someone who consciously makes the universal as such into the end of his activity, merely through his participation in civil society, even though individuals can come to pursue in a self-conscious way the common good that is produced as an unintended consequence of the self-interest which animates civil society.[7] The corporation serves, in fact, as a good example of this; for although a corporation may have come into being through its members seeking to further their own interests, with the effective pursuit of these interests demanding that they join forces with others, such qualities as commitment and self-sacrifice will undoubtedly be required if the corporation is to be made to fulfil its original purpose. Yet, however significant this change of consciousness might be, the common good that is consciously willed in this way can still be explained in terms of self-interest, and does not require that individuals consciously identify themselves with ethical life as a whole.

Hegel therefore needs to explain how modern ethical life involves a unity of the subjective will and the universal will which does not imply the kind of external relation that characterizes their relation to each other in civil society; and by so doing he might also be able to explain why individuals should adopt the standpoint of the *citoyen* as well as that of the *bourgeois*. This standpoint relates to a feature of ethical life which for Hegel is common to both its ancient and its modern forms: the idea that the union of the individual will with the universal will takes place not for the sake of particular ends but for the sake of union as such (VRP 2 210). In other words, the individual is here thought of as someone who identifies with the universal (i.e. the ethical whole) as such and consciously makes it – and not just his own private interests or the corporate interests of any group to which he belongs – into the end of his activity. Although this suggests that Hegel wants to make the transition from a negative concept of freedom (i.e. freedom of choice) to a positive one, he does not thereby end up equating what individuals would choose if they were rational with what they actually choose, as one of his liberal critics would have it.[8] For, as I have already shown, he clearly thinks that individuals can entertain a purely negative conception of freedom and that this conception of freedom is an integral feature of the modern world, even though, as we shall see, it fails in his view to explain the possibility of the good life as it might be led in the modern state.

Although the type of insight based on good, but essentially instrumental, reasons fails to fully explain the unity of the subjective will and the universal will in a way that is commensurate with the idea of moral autonomy, Hegel speaks of a higher form of insight when he claims that it is only for rational cognition that the universal is the end and the particular only the means to this end (VRP 2 151). He also claims that an adequate cognition of the identity in which 'the ethical is the actual living principle of self-consciousness' belongs to conceptual thought (PR §147A). At the same time, Hegel concedes that not everyone will attain the level of philosophical cognition: for while one person might demand of himself only that his insight into an obligation should be based on good reasons, another person might additionally demand of himself that he should recognize this obligation in terms of its concept (PR §132A). These remarks tell us that for Hegel an essentially conceptual form of insight is available into the rationality of modern ethical life, and this invites the question as to the precise nature of this conceptual form of knowledge.

Part of the answer to this question lies in the notion of necessity, which, together with universality, is for Hegel the mark of what is rational. For Hegel, reflective thought in general therefore involves the demand that the necessity of its content should be shown (EL §1). In the case of his own system of right, this necessity is to be found in the way in which it arises through the '*immanent* progression and production of its own determinations', which is 'assumed to be familiar from logic' (PR §31). In other words, the determinations of Hegel's system of right arise through a dialectical process, in which one determination reveals itself to be inadequate in some way and gives rise to a higher determination in which this limitation is overcome. This invites the question as to the extent to which the immanent progression and production of its own determinations that for Hegel takes place in his philosophy of right depends on another aspect of objectivity which he identifies in his discussion of this term.

Unlike Kant, Hegel thinks that the essential structure of reality as it is in itself can be known theoretically; he therefore claims that the term 'objectivity' also signifies 'the *In-itself* as thought-product, the significance of what is there, as distinct from what is only thought by us, and hence still distinct from the matter itself [*der Sache selbst*], or from the matter *in-itself*' (EL §41 Z2). Hegel attempts to provide an account and proof of the structure of this 'in-itself' in his logic. Since all reality must be thought to share the same basic underlying structure, it seems that this logical structure must also underlie Hegel's system of right; and one might therefore assume that the necessity exhibited by the determinations of Hegel's system of right ultimately needs to be explained in terms of his logic.

As far as the relation between his system of right and his logic is concerned, Hegel states in the preface to the published version of his philosophy of right that although he has omitted to demonstrate and bring out the logical progression in each and every detail on account of the concrete and inherently varied nature of the subject matter, both the work as a whole and the construction of its parts are based on the 'logical spirit'. This statement throws little light on the relation between the philosophy of right and Hegel's logic, however; for it does not imply that the structure of the former is determined by the structure of the latter, rather than its first undergoing its own immanent development which can, on reflection, be seen to correspond to certain essential features of Hegel's logic. For instance, although Hegel claims that the constitution of the political state is rational in so far as it '*differentiates* and determines its activity within itself *in accordance with the nature of the concept*' (PR §272), he might only mean that the political state shows itself to divide into three elements (i.e. the legislature, the executive, and the constitutional monarchy), which can then be seen to correspond to the three moments of the concept of his logic (i.e. universality, particularity, and individuality). Moreover, in this particular case any attempt to link Hegel's philosophy of right to his logic faces the problem that when Hegel comes to present his dialectical exposition of the political state, he in fact inverts the logical order by beginning with the monarch instead of the legislature.[9]

The prospect of seeking the highest form of insight into the rationality of modern ethical life in Hegel's logic does not therefore seem to be an especially promising one. In what follows, we shall discover that Hegel's remarks on the relation between the concept of the will and the concept of right suggest another way in which there might be a conceptual form of knowledge that provides individuals with insight into the unity of their own subjective wills and the universal will embodied in the various determinations of modern ethical life. The explanation that Hegel thus gives of the unity of the subjective will and the universal will can be viewed, moreover, as a specifically modern one, deriving from the modern natural law tradition, whose implications Hegel seeks to develop even though he criticizes some of the main ideas associated with this tradition, such as the idea of a social contract.

Right as Objectified Will

We saw in Chapter 1 that Hegel describes a transition from individual self-consciousness to the universal self-consciousness of spirit as taking place in his *Encyclopaedia* philosophy of subjective spirit. In this universal self-consciousness, individuals demonstrate their recognition of others as being of the same general type as themselves by limiting their own activity in relation to them, thus leaving open to others a sphere in which they can effectively exercise free choice and determine themselves as individuals. Universal self-consciousness can in this respect be held to be the condition of individual self-consciousness in two senses: the recognition granted by others confirms one's understanding of oneself as an independent being; and, since this recognition takes the form of each person limiting his activity in relation to others, it also allows each person to determine himself as an individual distinct from other individuals through the exercise of free choice.

Although Hegel's theory of universal self-consciousness in this way represents a theory concerning the type of being that is capable of standing in relations of right to others, he does not treat the concept of right as the immediate result of this universal self-consciousness; and it is therefore incorrect to state that Hegel's deduction of right is given in the section on universal self-consciousness.[10] There is, moreover, a perfectly good explanation for Hegel's unwillingness to directly link the concept of universal self-consciousness with the concept of right, which makes its appearance only later in the *Encyclopaedia* in the section on objective spirit. This explanation concerns the fact that Hegel provides an account of the will before he introduces the concept of right and subsequent to his account of universal self-consciousness; for this shows that he considers the concept of the will to be so integral to his philosophy of right, which develops the section on objective spirit found in the *Encyclopaedia*, that its necessity must first be demonstrated and its essential nature determined before the concept of right can be introduced. It is consequently better to speak of Hegel's demonstration of a 'generic consciousness' as providing only the negative conditions of the concept of right, whereas his positive conception of right is to be found in his understanding of the latter as the existence of the free and rational will.[11] I now intend to look more closely at how Hegel establishes a vital link between the concept of the will and the concept of right, and to explain his reasons for thinking that he is thereby able to explain the unity of the subjective will and the universal will which constitutes the essence of ethical life.

Hegel describes right in terms that serve to emphasize the idea that it is as much a product of the will as a limitation on it, as when he calls his system of right 'the realm of actualized freedom' (PR §4) and the 'system of self-actualizing freedom' (VRP 2 52). Hegel thus explains the identity of right and the subjective will of the individual in terms of the idea that the latter's freedom is given a concrete, abiding and non-contingent form in the various determinations of right which make up his theory of modern ethical life. The identity in question accords with Kant's idea of moral autonomy, which constitutes a type of relation in which the ethical norms to which an individual is subject are equally expressions of this same individual's rational will. For right is likewise an expression of one's own subjective will, whose essential nature is freedom, which is therefore just as much a basic determination of the will as weight is a basic determination of bodies (PR §4Z). At the same time, the determinations of right, as publicly known laws and institutions, have the kind of external existence which allows individuals to gain an intuition of their freedom in them; and this is why Hegel describes right as any existence [*Dasein*] in general which is the existence of the free will (PR §29). He therefore claims that right should not be understood as referring only to limited juridical laws, but should instead be understood as the existence of all the determinations of freedom (EG §486). We must now look more closely at Hegel's account of the will and its relation to the concept of right so as to discover exactly how right constitutes the existence of the free will.

Hegel's conception of right as the expression and realization of human freedom, as opposed to its being merely a limitation on natural freedom and the arbitrary will, is evident from the way in which the concept of the will forms the point of departure for his exposition of the various determinations of right (PR §4), in which he seeks to specify the conditions under which human freedom can be fully realized. Although Hegel's philosophy of right is therefore to be viewed as a theory of self-realization, the claim that his system of right specifies the conditions under which human freedom can be fully realized is an ambiguous one because it can be interpreted in a strong or a weak sense. The stronger claim would be that the determinations of modern ethical life are the conditions of subjectivity itself, that is to say, the conditions of being able to understand oneself as an independent, reflective, self-conscious agent;[12] for this makes it sound as if subjectivity itself would not be possible in the absence of the laws and institutions of modern ethical life, in the sense that it simply could not have developed in their absence. Such an interpretation of Hegel's philosophy of right appears to ignore the distinction which he makes between formal freedom and 'substantial' freedom, however.

As we have seen, Hegel's account of self-consciousness features the idea of the capacity to conceive of oneself in abstraction from all given determinations, including the norms and social relations that characterize the social world to which one just happens to belong. Individuals with this capacity are therefore to some extent independent of this social world, in the sense that they are able to assume a reflective attitude towards it. The self-certainty in question is, however, only a formal kind of freedom, distinct from the substantial freedom which consists in having an intuition of one's freedom in the shape of the publicly known laws and institutions of modern ethical life, which at the same time are the source of an individual's various duties, so that in performing these duties individuals can potentially experience a sense of liberation rather than constraint (PR §149).

In the light of this distinction between formal freedom and substantial freedom it is possible to conceive of individuals who are free in the former sense of the term, and thus have the character of subjects, but not in the latter sense. Socrates is a case in point, for Hegel clearly regards him as an independent, reflective, self-conscious agent who happened to live, however, in a time of social decay (PR §138Z). Indeed, Hegel's claim that subjective reflection was first introduced into the world by the Sophists and Socrates looks highly problematic if we understand such reflection to be dependent on the nature of one's social world.[13] Moreover, Hegel associates both Socrates and the Stoics with the tendency to seek truth within oneself, which obviously requires an independent reflective attitude in times which, as Hegel himself puts it, 'the existing world of freedom has become unfaithful to the better will' (PR §138A).

Although the examples given above suggest that it may only be exceptional individuals who are able to develop and maintain a conception of themselves as independent, reflective, self-conscious agents in the face of a social world which does not reflect and promote such an understanding of oneself, they nevertheless show that Hegel does not think that such a self-understanding absolutely depends on the existence of the right kind of laws and institutions. After all, how should laws and institutions that promote an understanding of oneself as a reflective and independent being have developed if some people had not already developed such an understanding of themselves and thus felt the need to transform their social world in accordance with this new understanding of themselves?

This brings me to the weaker version of the interpretation of Hegel's philosophy of right as a theory of self-realization. This would involve the idea that it is possible to be an independent, reflective, self-conscious agent even in a society which lacked the laws and institutions that make up modern ethical life; yet, in the absence of these laws and institutions, the agent in question must experience his social world as something alien to himself since it does not provide the conditions for the proper exercise and development of the capacities associated with his understanding of himself as a free and reflective agent. In this respect, the various determinations of Hegel's system of right must be held to be the necessary conditions of the full development and maintenance of such an understanding of oneself, but not the necessary conditions of this self-understanding itself.

Hegel thinks that this experience of one's social world as being alien to oneself can be fully overcome in the case of modern ethical life because individuals are in principle able to gain insight into the rationality of its laws and institutions in a way that demonstrates the identity of their own subjective wills with these determinations of right. As we shall now see, the reason for this is that right can, according to Hegel, be viewed as the concrete expression and objectification of the general will and as possessing validity only in virtue of this fact. This is not to say, however, that Hegel's conception of the general will accords with the way in which it has traditionally been understood in social contract theory, that is, as a collective will which is generated through individuals consenting to submit themselves to the conditions that it imposes upon them.

Hegel's conception of the general, or universal, will instead relates to his account of the concept of the will; for he states in connection with Rousseau's distinction between the general will and the will of all that the general will (*der allgemeine Wille*) is the concept of the will (*der Begriff des Willens*) (EL §163Z1). Consequently, the will which forms the subject of Hegel's philosophy of right, in the sense of both its subject matter and its organizing principle, is not, strictly speaking, to be identified with the subjective will of the individual. This general will must instead be viewed as the concept of the will as such, that is, the general will which Hegel introduces only after having purged it of all incidental causal determinations in his *Encylopaedia* theory of subjective spirit.[14] In other words, the general or universal will is to be understood as the concept of the will instantiated in each and every subjective will.

By identifying the general will with what is already essential to each and every subjective will, Hegel avoids some of the main problems associated with the idea of the general will in social contract theory, such as the problem as to how a genuinely universally valid will can be thought to arise from the composition of many individual wills, whose particular interests may in fact corrupt the general will or even rule out the possibility of generating it in the first place. This approach also allows Hegel to avoid basing the authority of the state on the kind of arbitrary decision which in Fichte's contract theory of the state appears to reduce the relation between the subjective will and the universal will to a purely contingent or 'external' one. Hegel, by contrast, seeks to explain the unity of the subjective will of the individual and the universal will embodied in the various determinations of right in terms of the way in which modern ethical life constitutes the concrete expression and existence of the general will which forms the essence, or concept, of each and every subjective will.

While this interpretation of Hegel's theory of right confirms the view that his conception of freedom does not constitute an abandonment of the voluntarist tradition of modern political philosophy, but rather represents the most radical and self-consistent expression of the modern emphasis on the primacy of the will,[15] we are now able to state precisely in what sense Hegel radicalizes this tradition, namely by reinterpreting one of its central ideas, the general will, in terms of the concept of the will that he holds to be essential to each and every individual will. In this respect, Hegel can also be seen as attempting to make the voluntarist tradition of modern political philosophy more consistent by explaining the possibility of a genuinely universal will, which does not first need to be constructed through the composition of many individual wills, as is still suggested by Kant's description of the general will of the people as a united one, even though he views the social contract in hypothetical terms. Yet even if Hegel thus removes the ambiguity which still attaches to Kant's conception of the general will, Hegel's own approach itself invites another problem faced by social contract theory: the problem as to what would count as an adequate expression of the general will. As we shall see below, Hegel's proposed solution to this problem relates to the idea that his system of right is the concrete expression and existence of the concept of the will, though I shall argue that Hegel may have recognized that modern ethical life suffers from certain significant limitations in this respect. We must therefore now look more closely at Hegel's account of the concept of the will, so as to gain a better understanding of the way in which the various determinations of right that make up his theory of modern ethical life constitute the concrete expression and existence of this concept.

For Hegel, the concept of the will comprises three moments, with the third moment consisting in the unity of the two other moments. He describes the first moment of the will as one of '*pure indeterminacy* or of the "I" 's pure reflection into itself, in which every limitation, every content ... is dissolved' (PR §5). This is clearly a description of subjectivity in the sense of the abstract self-certainty of the 'I' = 'I', which involves conceiving of oneself in abstraction from all one's determinations and regarding oneself as independent of them, thus making one aware of one's capacity to exercise free choice. This form of freedom is, however, one-sided because the will cannot be an actual will unless it posits something determinate as its content and object. In other words, in order to have a will in the proper sense of the term, the subject must will something determinate and thus lose its abstract universality. Consequently, Hegel calls the second moment of the will 'the absolute moment of the *finitude* or *particularization* of the "I" ' (PR §6). This second moment of the will can also be related to Hegel's account of subjectivity because it corresponds to the way in which the exercise of free choice allows a person to determine himself as an individual person distinct from others in virtue of the different choices that he makes. Finally, since both the moment of pure indeterminacy and the moment of particularization are essential features of the will, the concept of the latter is the unity of these two moments, a unity which allows the 'I' to remain with itself (*bei sich*) even in the act of positing itself 'as the negative of itself, that is, as *determinate* and *limited*'

(PR §7). In other words, the 'I' remains self-determining because the content of its willing is an object of its freedom of choice.

In spite of its self-determining character, the concept of the will is subject to a significant limitation, however; for, as Hegel himself puts it: 'This unity is the will *in itself* or *for us*. It is free will, however, inasmuch as it makes itself into its object and content, and thus wills itself, i.e. so long as it wills to be free. Thus is it *for itself* what it is *in itself*' (VRP 1 39). The idea behind this claim relates to another meaning of the term 'subjectivity' which Hegel identifies, namely, that which is subjective in the sense of belonging to the realm of thought alone (PR §25). An example of subjectivity in this sense of the term would be the arbitrary will in so far as it makes a choice but does not act upon it or is prevented from doing so. Hegel extends this idea to the concept of the will itself, which, as merely a concept, remains an object of thought alone, whereas right constitutes the actual existence of this concept. The various determinations of Hegel's theory of modern ethical life therefore represent necessary moments in the actualization of the concept of the will, a process which culminates in the will's embodiment in a set of laws and institutions which are unified in the idea of the state understood in the broader sense of the term that I mentioned in the previous chapter. At the level of modern ethical life, the content of the will is thus a determinate one, whereas at the level of abstract right and morality it remains largely a matter of contingency or at best involves what remain merely abstract ideas such as happiness, the welfare of all and duty.

Although Hegel does not take the particular will of the individual as the point of departure for his philosophy of right, as he believes social contract theory does, it is necessary for him to describe how the moment of the particularity of the will in all its forms, including the natural will and the arbitrary will, is objectified in his system of right, since the particularization or finitude of the will constitutes an essential moment of the concept of the will. The fact that certain determinations of right, especially the laws and institutions of civil society, are essentially related to the will in its particularity and finitude does not therefore mean that the subject of Hegel's philosophy of right is not a general will, in the sense of the concept of the will contained in each and every subjective will; for this general will itself requires the objectification of the particularity of the will in a set of laws and institutions. In this respect, the actualization of the second moment of the will, in so far as it concerns the particularity of the will, can be seen to take place at two different levels in the philosophy of right: at the level of the subjective will in the case of abstract right and morality, as when the initially abstract person seeks to determine himself as a particular individual through the exercise of free choice and the moral subject demands that its welfare is taken into consideration; and at the level of modern ethical life, which contains a set of laws and institutions that realize the right of the subjective will and guarantee individuals the right to exercise free choice. Moreover, the objectification of the concept of the will in a set of laws and institutions provides another example of how the second moment of the will is realized in Hegel's philosophy of right because these laws and institutions can be understood to represent both the particularization of the will and, since they are historically conditioned, the finitude of the will.

The way in which the concept of the will constitutes the subject of Hegel's philosophy of right provides another reason, in addition to the idea that individuals produce the ethical substance through their own activity, for thinking that the unity of the subjective will and the universal will is the essence of ethical life. For the determinations of modern ethical life can now be seen to form the objective aspect of that of which the concept of the will forms the subjective aspect, namely human freedom. Individuals do not, therefore, need to think of the laws and institutions of modern ethical life merely as setting limits, albeit necessary and legitimate ones, to their freedom of choice: they can instead think of them as the expression and existence of their own wills. This identity of the subjective will and the universal will means, moreover, that individuals are able to think of this universal will as not being alien to them. In short, we appear to have a relation of the universal will to the subjective will which accords with both the idea of moral autonomy and Hegel's understanding of freedom as the will's being with itself in its other through which it gains an intuition of itself. This helps to explain Hegel's claim that the subject stands in a relationship to the ethical substance and its laws and powers which is immediate and closer to identity than a relationship of faith or trust, even though we have seen that this identity is typically a highly mediated one in the case of modern ethical life, which also allows individuals to experience the satisfaction of their particularity.

Hegel's conception of right as the concrete expression of the general will contained in each and every subjective will means that modern ethical life as a whole, and not only one or more of its determinations (e.g. the family and the corporation) taken in isolation from the others, must be taken to form the content that individuals need to will in order to become fully free. Hegel himself speaks of the absolute drive of the free spirit to have its own freedom as its object, so that the abstract concept of the idea of the will is the free will which wills the free will (PR §27), and we can now identify this free will as being one that must ultimately will the actualization of its own concept in the shape of the laws and institutions of modern ethical life. Since people will need to actualize and sustain this set of laws and institutions through their own theoretical and practical activity, each individual will have an incentive for making the universal as such (i.e. modern ethical life as a whole) into the end of his activity, that is to say, an incentive for adopting the standpoint of the *citoyen* as well as that of the *bourgeois*.[16] Although this appears to turn the relation of the subjective will to the universal will into an instrumental, and hence merely 'external', one, the content of the will is not this time one possible end among others; it is instead a content that Hegel considers to be essential to the will itself, namely, freedom. An unwillingness to take seriously the idea that one's social world may or may not be an adequate expression of human freedom could therefore be taken to imply a lack of seriousness concerning the realization of one's own freedom.

Although the *bourgeois* in this way has good reasons for adopting the standpoint of the *citoyen*, the idea that an instrumental or prudential attitude alone may motivate individuals to act in conformity with right is nevertheless compatible with Hegel's description of the modern form of virtue, rectitude, as simply doing what is required of one; for this conception of virtue does not imply that what actually motivates individuals to act in conformity with right is of any real importance. Individuals may therefore be motivated solely by an insight based on good reasons which has its ultimate basis in private interest; and it is consequently possible to think of people doing no more than the bare minimum required of them in relation to their various social roles so as to avoid certain sanctions or to realize their own personal ends, such as the wish to enjoy a certain type of lifestyle. The way in which Hegel views right as objectified will nevertheless suggests, I believe, that individuals have a reason for performing their social roles with a sense of commitment and thus in a way that involves doing more than the bare minimum that is required of them.[17]

The reason in question relates to the fact that the social whole to which individuals belong is, for Hegel, the condition of the full realization of everyone's freedom, including each individual's own freedom, and to the idea that the laws and institutions of the state can function properly only through the conscious activity of its individual members. For, when taken together, these two aspects of ethical life suggest that a genuine sense of commitment will be needed if these laws and institutions, which form the conditions of the full realization of human freedom, are to become fully actual, with regard to both their existence and their effective operation. Consequently, although it might be possible to conceive of a society in which people do the bare minimum required of them, it can be asked whether such a society could be classed as a good one in comparison with a society in which individuals feel fully committed to their social roles and experience a sense of duty in relation to them. In short, a condition in which individuals are fully committed to their social roles because they identify themselves with them appears to realize the idea of the good life better than a condition in which people tend to think of their social world as having a merely instrumental function and do not feel the need to do more than the minimum required of them.

In this respect, Hegel's theory of modern ethical life can be seen to represent an attempt on his part to demonstrate that freedom and rationality not only make a condition of right possible, but also can themselves only become fully actual in the type of community of free and rational beings standing in relations of right to each other which he calls ethical life; and this is why he claims that it is by living together in an ethical way that human beings achieve liberation and arrive at an intuition of themselves (VRP 2 125). At the same time, Hegel wants to incorporate the reflective form of consciousness that he associates with subjectivity into his theory of modern ethical life and to meet the various demands that arise in connection with the principle of subjective freedom; and he therefore incorporates some important elements of Kant's and Fichte's thought, in which the principle of subjectivity finds philosophical expression, and the modern natural law tradition in general, into his philosophy of right.[18]

There remains, however, an important issue which I have not addressed in connection with Hegel's conception of right as objectified will because my main aim has been to demonstrate that his philosophy of right is motivated by the project of situating subjectivity within a framework of universally valid ethical norms. I believe that this project is a largely coherent one which is grounded on a fully worked-out theory of subjectivity, one that treats the latter both in purely conceptual terms and as an historical phenomenon. The idea of such a project invites the question, however, as to whether or not the specific determinations of Hegel's system of right can in fact be held to constitute truly adequate objectifications of the general will understood as the concept of the will contained in each and every subjective will. One could perhaps argue that even if some, or even most, of these determinations of right cannot be understood as necessary objectifications of the general will present in each and every subjective will, we do not for this reason have to reject the basic project that lies behind Hegel's philosophy of right. Yet there are tensions within the latter that are related to the project of situating subjectivity within a framework of universally valid ethical norms and Hegel's conception of right as objectified will; so that the idea of separating this project from the actual details of Hegel's theory of modern ethical life turns out to be more difficult than it at first appears.

I now intend to show, in fact, that Hegel's attempt to realize the project of situating subjectivity within a framework of universally valid ethical norms and his conception of right as objectified will when taken together imply a lack of unity between the subjective will of the individual and the universal will in the case of those individuals who are the victims of poverty, so that these individuals would be justified in acting in opposition to the universal will. In other words, Hegel must concede that certain members of the modern state have a right of rebellion. I shall argue that this right derives from the emphasis that Hegel places on the idea that right is as much an expression of human freedom as a limitation on it, as becomes evident if we compare Kant's position on the issue of the right of rebellion to the one that can reasonably be attributed to Hegel, with Hegel's theory of right proving to have more radical implications than Kant's theory of it.

Chapter 5: Kant and Hegel on the Right of Rebellion

Kant on the Right of Rebellion

Both Kant and Hegel have been linked to a particular revolution, the French Revolution, on the grounds that certain features of their thought are in harmony with this historical event.[1] In Kant's case, this apparent harmony between philosophical theory and historical event appears to make him guilty of a 'curious discrepancy' when he rejects the idea of a people's right to rebel against the established authorities.[2] Hegel, on the other hand, does not explicitly reject the idea that such a right exists; nor, however, does he deal specifically with the question as to whether people would, in certain circumstances, have a right of rebellion. Dieter Henrich nevertheless argues that Hegel allows that the poor have the right to rebel because the way in which society is organized prevents them from realizing their freedom.

In order to justify this claim, Henrich appeals to the following passage from Hegel's 1819/20 lectures on the philosophy of right, in which Hegel concerns himself with the plight of the poor: 'We earlier considered the right of necessity [*das Notrecht*] in relation to a momentary need. Here necessity [*Not*] no longer has this merely momentary character' (VRP 2 196). For Hegel, the right of necessity can be invoked when a person is forced to infringe another person's property rights so as to preserve his own life, as when, for example, he steals a loaf of bread in order not to starve (PR §127). Henrich suggests that the abiding character which the right of necessity assumes in the case of the poor shows that, for Hegel, the hardship (*Not*) associated with poverty is a result of the very way in which society is organized, so that the existing social order does not allow the poor to give existence (*Dasein*) to their wills, which therefore remain unrealized.[3] As we shall see, this amounts to the poor being unable to experience the realization of their own freedom, so that they would be justified in rebelling against the existing social order.

It has been argued that Henrich perhaps exaggerates the radical character of Hegel's social and political philosophy by reading too much into a single passage, and that Hegel can hardly be said to have had in mind the idea that the whole bourgeois system of civil society should be overthrown and replaced with something different.[4] The last point is certainly a valid one because civil society performs the essential function of accommodating subjective freedom within modern ethical life and thereby provides individuals with an insight based on good reasons into the rationality of the laws and institutions of the modern state. I nevertheless intend to argue in what follows that Hegel's conception of right as objectified will implies that the poor do indeed have a right of rebellion because society, in virtue of the way in which it is organized, prevents them from giving existence to their own subjective wills.

The fact that Hegel must concede that the poor have a right of rebellion and his commitment to the view that civil society is a necessary feature of modern ethical life are thus a source of tension within his philosophy of right, a tension which stems from his conception of right as objectified will and his attempt to incorporate the principle of subjective freedom into his theory of modern ethical life. In what follows, although I intend to adopt a different approach from Henrich's, I shall reach the same conclusion as he does, though this time one that is not based on the idea of a right of necessity but on Hegel's attempt to come to terms with the principle of subjective freedom. I should point out, however, that I do not mean to suggest that Hegel explicitly asserts a right of rebellion in the case of the poor; my point is rather that such a right can reasonably be deduced from certain central features of his philosophy of right, so that even though Hegel did not himself draw the conclusion that the poor have a right of rebellion, he should have done so.

Although my main intention is to show that Hegel must concede that the poor have a right of rebellion, or, to be exact, that he provides no grounds for denying them this right but some grounds for granting them such a right, I shall begin with a brief look at Kant's denial of the right of rebellion, since this will allow me to introduce an issue that will help to identify why Hegel must grant a right of rebellion to the poor. The issue in question concerns the source of the legitimacy of the state and its various determinations, by means of which it gains its authority in relation to its citizens, who therefore have no right to rebel against it. I shall again briefly mention Kant's views on how the legitimacy of the state and its laws is to be established and relate them to his rejection of the idea of a right of rebellion. I shall point out, however, that Kant would clearly have to concede that people would in certain circumstances be justified in rebelling against the established authorities. I shall then turn to Hegel's philosophy of right so as to show that he can be seen to provide the determinations of his theory of right with legitimacy in a way that both mirrors and differs from Kant's attempt to do the same thing. Finally, I shall argue that Hegel's different conception of right and his version of the idea of a general will commit him to a more radical position on the issue of the right of rebellion than the one that can be attributed to Kant on this issue.

As we have seen, the concept of personality is fundamental to Kant's theory of right because the latter primarily serves as the means of protecting the rights that derive from one's having the status of a person. These rights include the right not to unjustly suffer physical harm, the right to pursue one's own personal ends, as long as one does not thereby unjustly prevent others from pursuing their own ends, and the right to maintain possession of or to alienate any legitimately acquired items of property that one may own. For Kant, these rights can only be secured by the civil constitution, so that the legitimacy of the laws of the state must be seen to derive from the way in which they guarantee the rights stemming from one's status as a person. Kant assumes, moreover, that such laws are therefore conditions which all individuals could reasonably be expected to impose upon themselves.

Kant's basic objection to the idea that people have a right of rebellion is tied up with this view of the civil constitution's primary function. It also involves an appeal to the principle of universalization, which demands that one must be able to universalize the maxim upon which one intends to act. Kant argues that in the case of a right of rebellion, the universalization of the maxim upon which the individual intends to act would result in a contradiction because it must lead to the destruction of the whole civil constitution and thus to the disappearance of the only condition in which all individuals can have rights (TP 299/81). In other words, the universalization of the maxim which expresses the idea of a right of rebellion is expressed would ultimately lead to people losing their rights altogether, since these rights can only be guaranteed by the civil constitution, which would, however, be destroyed through the act of rebellion. Whereas in the state of nature, which would return in the wake of the destruction of the civil constitution, there would be no judge competent to render a verdict which could then be enforced should any dispute arise concerning a person's claim to possess the right to a thing or to the performance or non-performance of an action (MS 312). Each person would, in short, end up being the judge of his or her own cause. Similarly, if the civil constitution itself contained an article which permitted the people to resist the sovereign power, there would be no independent judge competent to render a verdict should a dispute arise between the sovereign and the people (MS 319–20).

Kant thus appears to assume two things: first of all, that individuals possess rights and, secondly, that such rights can only be secured by the civil constitution, which cannot, moreover, contain an article that would permit the people to resist the sovereign for this would bring into question the civil constitution's ability to perform this same function. With respect to the first assumption, we already know that it is based on Kant's view of persons as having the moral status of ends in themselves, and that this conception of personality also forms an essential feature of Hegel's account of what it means to be a person. With respect to the second assumption, Hegel's account of civil society and its relation to the political state shows that he also holds the view that the rights which derive from one's having the status of a person can only be secured by the laws and institutions of the state.

Even if, for the sake of argument, we accept that Kant has demonstrated the moral foundations of the civil constitution, so that to rebel against it would be immoral, this does not appear to warrant the conclusion that it would always be wrong to rebel against the established authorities. For by giving the state a moral foundation, Kant commits himself to the idea that the state must fulfil its moral function in order to possess legitimacy; nor is he blind to the fact that certain states, or even each and every existing state, may lack legitimacy in this respect; and in such cases he proposes a process of gradual reform prompted by public criticism.[5] This presupposes that such public criticism is possible within a society, however; yet in a totalitarian state, with its lack of respect for the rule of law and its suppression of any signs of dissent, public criticism would not be possible. Such a condition may therefore be considered to be worse than a state of anarchy; and the state can thus be viewed as having violated the original contract from which it derived its legitimacy.[6] One can, in short, imagine a situation in which the state completely fails to perform the moral function from which it gains its legitimacy, so that it would no longer be immoral to rebel against it. Although this shows that Kant must concede that a right of rebellion exists in cases when the state does not respect his universal law of right, which guarantees the rights of persons by setting limits to the exercise of free choice, I now intend to argue that Hegel must concede that a right of rebellion may exist even when the universal law of right is respected, so that in this respect his philosophy of right turns out to have more radical implications than Kant's theory of right.

Hegel on the Right of Rebellion

In order to understand why Hegel must be thought to allow that a right of rebellion exists even when the state has the character of a Kantian *Rechtstaat*, we need to remember that the legitimacy of the various determinations of the civil constitution for Kant rests on the fact that these determinations can be understood as expressions of the general will, that is, as conditions which individuals may reasonably impose upon both themselves and others. Hegel adopts a similar view of the matter with regard to the source of the legitimacy of the various determinations that make up his system of right, since he considers these determinations to be objectifications of the general will (i.e. the concept of the will instantiated in each and every individual will). Yet in so doing, Hegel offers a markedly different theory of right from the one offered by Kant, for he is able to emphasize that right is as much an expression of the free will as a limitation, albeit a necessary and thus legitimate one, on natural freedom and the arbitrary will, which is how Kant for the most part seems to view right.

Hegel's system of right must therefore be seen to constitute the complete objectification of the free will. In other words, it comprises a set of laws and institutions all of which must be in place if the various aspects of human freedom are to be realized. These aspects of human freedom include freedom of choice, which rests upon the will's abstract universality, but they also include the second moment of the will, which involves the act of resolving upon one content of the will rather than another, so that the will in this sense particularizes itself and becomes an actual will. This particularization of the will can be understood in two different ways, however: in the case of any single individual will, it can be identified with the act of making one thing rather than another into the content of one's will through the exercise of free choice; whereas at the more general level of the concept of the will as such, it can be identified with this concept's objectification in a set of laws and institutions. The second sense in which the will particularizes itself thus relates to Hegel's theory of right as objectified will, while the first sense in which it particularizes itself concerns the arbitrary will. It is this dual conception of the second moment of the will that appears to commit Hegel to the view that a right of rebellion must be granted to the poor even when the state has achieved the form of a Kantian *Rechtstaat*, as I shortly intend to demonstrate in relation to some of Hegel's remarks on the problems of poverty and social alienation.

The necessity which Hegel attaches to the will's need to particularize itself so as to become an actual will commits him to explaining how the arbitrary will finds its place within his system of right. As we saw in Chapter 3, civil society is the sphere of modern ethical life which allows individuals to exercise free choice and forms the context within which these individuals, in their mutual dependence, satisfy their natural and non-natural needs. However, as I have already pointed out, the fact that certain determinations of right are essentially connected with the will in its particularity does not mean that the subject of Hegel's philosophy of right is not a general will. On the contrary, as the concept of the will found in each and every subjective will, the general will contains the moment of finitude or particularization within itself, and thus gives rise to the demand to provide the will in its particularity with its corresponding determinations of right (i.e. the laws and institutions of civil society).

We saw that the satisfaction of the individual's particularity requires laws and institutions whose function is to protect the common interest that arises on the basis of the condition of mutual dependence which Hegel calls the system of needs, including the legal system, before which all individuals are considered to be equal, and the public authority, which enforces the laws and regulations that set limits to the exercise of free choice, thus guaranteeing the rights of all members of civil society. These laws and regulations in turn refer us beyond civil society itself to the political state, which constitutes the sphere of modern ethical life in which these laws and regulations are drawn up and the best means of applying or implanting them are decided upon. Civil society, in its relation to the political state, is, in short, the sphere of modern ethical life in which Kant's universal law of right becomes actual. This universal law of right, which is based on the idea of personality, guarantees the legal status of persons, and, by treating all persons as equal, it requires abstracting from any differences between them. In this respect, civil society serves to realize the first moment of the will, the moment of abstract universality; for, as Marx puts it, '*Equality* is nothing but a translation into French, i.e. into political form, of the German "*Ich* = *Ich*".'[7] We saw in Chapter 3, moreover, that Hegel's theory of civil society has much in common with Kant's *Rechtstaat*, with regard to both its function and the source of the legitimacy of its various laws and institutions, in so far as this sphere of modern ethical life serves to realize the concept of personality. I shall argue below, however, that although Kant's *Rechtstaat* realizes the first moment of the will, it fails to fully realize the second moment, whereas Hegel thinks that this moment of the will must also be realized in the modern state if the latter is to be an adequate expression of the general will.

Hegel's view of the particularity of the will as an essential moment of the concept of the will has some significant implications in connection with the problem of poverty, a problem which Hegel discusses in some detail, whereas Kant pays little attention to it. Kant attempts to deal with the problem of poverty in his theory of right when he argues that taxes may be imposed on the people for its own preservation and that these taxes may be used to provide for the poor because the general will of the people has united itself into a society that is to maintain itself perpetually, which will, he alleges, require supporting those who cannot support themselves (MS 326). The problem with this argument is that societies in which poverty constitutes a structural feature are arguably able to maintain themselves. In what follows, I intend to argue that Hegel's account of the concept of the will and his understanding of right as objectified will imply that such a state of affairs would undermine the state's claim to possess legitimacy, and that he must therefore allow that an act of rebellion against the existing social order may be justified even when Kant's universal law of right is recognized by the state. We shall see, in fact, that the problem of poverty brings into question civil society's capacity to perform the function of satisfying the will in its particularity, a function that Hegel considers to be essential because it helps to realize the second moment of the concept of the will.

I do not intend to go into the details of Hegel's account of poverty and social alienation. For present purposes it is enough to say that he states that poverty is a necessary consequence of civil society (VRP 2 193). By this he means that poverty is a direct result of the normal workings of the market economy which animates civil society, as in the case of the problem of overproduction, which occurs when the volume of goods produced lacks a corresponding number of consumers, so that workers must be laid off and are thus deprived of the means of supporting themselves and their families. Hegel does not appear to offer a definitive solution to the problem of poverty, however, even though he considers some possible solutions to this problem (PR §§242A, 245; VRP 4 611–12).[8] He also recognizes that poverty can lead to the loss of the feeling of right, integrity and honour which comes from supporting oneself through one's own activity, while the loss of these feelings may in turn result in a disposition that involves an inward rebellion against society, the rich, and the government, thus leading to the creation of a rabble (PR §244). Hegel claims, moreover, that a rabble forms when a large mass of people sinks below the level of a certain standard of living, with this standard automatically regulating itself at the level necessary for a member of the society in question (PR §244). In other words, he recognizes that poverty is relative because what is considered to be a condition of poverty in any given society will depend on such factors as how wealthy this society is.

Hegel can therefore be seen as having the following dilemma in mind: On the one hand, since they are necessary consequences of civil society, the problems of poverty and social alienation cannot be fully solved while civil society is allowed to operate according to its own distinctive principle, which is the principle of self-interest. On the other hand, it is not possible to abolish those features of civil society which give rise to the problems of poverty and social alienation, since these features are essential to civil society, which functions as the sphere of modern ethical life in which the right of the subject to experience the satisfaction of its particularity finds its realization. The right of the subject to experience the satisfaction of its particularity must, moreover, be realized within modern ethical life because the particularity of the will forms an essential moment of the general will which is objectified in Hegel's system of right. In this respect, it is certainly true to say that Hegel does not allow for the abolition of bourgeois civil society and its replacement by a system that could more adequately embody human freedom.

It is still the case, however, that the poor cannot be said to experience the objectification of the second moment of the will, the moment of particularization or finitude, as it relates to their own subjective wills, and they are therefore likely to experience a sense of alienation in relation to their social world, even if the latter has the form of the modern state outlined in Hegel's philosophy of right. We have seen, moreover, that for Hegel the satisfaction of their particularity provides individuals with a reason for identifying themselves with the interest of the state as a whole. Yet Hegel's account of the problems of poverty and social alienation suggests that he is also aware of the fact that in the modern state some individuals will be deprived of this reason for identifying themselves with their social world.

In some remarks that he makes concerning conditions in England, Hegel appears to concede that providing individuals with good reasons for identifying themselves with the interest of the state as a whole comes at the price of having to accept the problem of poverty and the rabble mentality to which it tends to give rise. For he identifies England as an example of the modern form of patriotism in which it is felt that one's own welfare is inextricably linked with the existence of the state (VRP 4 482); and yet, in the same series of lectures, he also describes England as follows: 'There is no other land in which so much is produced; no land which has such a [large] economy; and yet nowhere is poverty and the rabble mentality present to a greater and more terrible degree than in England' (VRP 4 611). As both the sphere of modern ethical life which accommodates the subject's right to experience the satisfaction of its particularity and the source of the problems of poverty and social alienation, civil society thus provides an example of how Hegel's attempt to accommodate the principle of subjective freedom within his system of right creates tensions within this system itself: for it now looks as if that which is meant to ensure that the subject's right to experience the satisfaction of its particularity is realized is itself the cause of some subjects not experiencing the satisfaction of their particularity.

This tension within Hegel's system of right clearly implies that modern ethical life, when viewed from the standpoint of the poor, does not constitute a fully adequate objectification of the concept of the will, so that the source of the state's legitimacy appears to conflict with social reality. The poor are, in fact, denied the two main forms of rational insight that Hegel thinks can be gained into the determinations of modern ethical life: the type of reason based on the realization that the modern state provides the best means of realizing one's personal ends and achieving happiness; and the insight into the identity of the subjective will and the universal will which consists in being able to recognize right as the objectification of the concept of the will contained in each and every subjective will, including one's own. In relation to the second form of insight, Hegel himself concedes that poverty gives rise to a sense of inner rebellion because 'the freedom of the individual has no existence [*Dasein*]', so that the recognition of universal freedom disappears (VPR 2 195). In other words, right, which for Hegel is as much an expression of human freedom as a limitation on it, is meant to be the concrete expression and existence of the concept of the will, which has particularity as one of its moments; yet the fact that some individuals do not experience the satisfaction of their particularity implies that they will not be able to experience their social world as an adequate expression of their own wills. Freedom in the fullest sense of the term is therefore not universally realized in the modern state, with the failure in question being due to the very nature of the modern state itself, which has the market economy as one of its constitutive features. Hegel's recognition of the problems of poverty and social alienation thus suggests that certain individuals within the modern state will be justified in claiming that the latter lacks the legitimacy which is held to derive from its being the concrete expression and existence of the general will understood as the concept of the will contained in each and every subjective will. Given this lack of legitimacy, the individuals in question would have the right to rebel against the existing social order in an attempt to bring about the true realization of their freedom.

The way in which a right of rebellion on the part of the poor turns out to be a consequence of Hegel's philosophy of right can be further illustrated with reference to his claim that both the Greeks and the Romans knew only that some are free, and not that man as such is free, whereas the Germanic nations, with the rise of Christianity, were the first to realize that 'man is by nature free, and that freedom of the spirit is his very essence' (VG 62/54). One reason for thinking that the Greeks and the Romans lacked the consciousness that man is by nature free is that they accepted the institution of slavery, which is based on the idea that certain people are essentially inferior to others; hence Aristotle's claim that any human being who 'by nature' belongs not to himself but to another is 'by nature' a slave.[9] In the modern state, by contrast, all individuals have the status of persons with certain inalienable rights, so that, as Hegel puts it, 'I am apprehended as a *universal* person, in which [respect] *all* are identical. A *human being counts as such because he is a human being*, not because he is a Jew, Catholic, Protestant, German, Italian, etc.' (PR §209A). The concept of personality is, in short, tied up with the idea of equality, of which equality before the law, the absence of privileges deriving from the circumstances of one's birth rather than from one's own efforts, and the right of each and every person to own property are particular expressions. In this respect, it is true to say that Hegel acclaimed the French Revolution because it helped what Kant calls the condition of right to achieve external existence.[10] The revolution in question must, however, be understood as the 'bourgeois' revolution, and not the revolution of the *sans-culottes*. There are nevertheless grounds for thinking that Hegel should have been sympathetic to both sides of the revolution, as becomes evident when we consider a distinction which he himself makes between the person and the human being, even though he does not always maintain this distinction.

We have seen that, for Hegel, the concept of the person unifies two different aspects of subjectivity: the abstract universality of the 'I' = 'I' and the finitude of the person who determines himself as an individual through the exercise of free choice. Both of these aspects of subjectivity find their corresponding objectifications in modern ethical life. While the abstract universality of the 'I' = 'I' finds its objectification in the legal system, before which everyone is held to be equal, and in the other ways in which the laws and institutions of civil society embody the idea of civil equality, the finite aspect of personality finds its objectification in civil society in so far as the latter not only allows the exercise of free choice and the pursuit of private interest, but also realizes the idea of welfare, both the welfare of the individual and the welfare of all.

Hegel sometimes appears to identify the concept of the person exclusively with the abstract universality of the 'I' = 'I', and thus with the first moment of the will, as when he claims that the simple abstraction 'person' has something contemptuous about it (PR §35Z). He also claims, however, that the system of needs starts out from the person in his entire particularity, and that it is the latter which we call a human being (VRP 2 152). Moreover it is only at the level of needs (i.e. civil society) that that which we call the human being becomes the object of right (PR §190A). Although it appears to go against Hegel's view of the person as a unity of the universal and particular aspects of subjectivity mentioned above, the distinction that Hegel thus appears to make between the person and the human being is a useful one in relation to the problem of poverty. For it implies that someone who is a victim of poverty possesses the status of a person, and consequently the rights associated with the idea of equality, which every member of the modern state can claim to enjoy, but does not enjoy the type of non-abstract freedom which Hegel associates with the human being, which requires the satisfaction of a whole set of needs, satisfaction that can only be achieved through one's active participation in civil society. In other words, the individual in question is denied many of the benefits that civil society has to offer, though not all of them.

The set of needs mentioned above must be thought to include the need for food, drink, clothing and shelter; for even if Hegel thinks that the capacity to determine oneself as an individual through the exercise of free choice by itself makes human beings into something more than merely natural beings, he also accepts that as a person I am myself an immediate individual, whose body forms the real possibility of any more determinate forms of existence (PR §190A). In other words, the exercise of free choice depends on the fact that I exist in my body because the latter enables me to realize my ends. This in turn means that I have a whole set of natural needs that demand to be satisfied before I can be in the position to effectively exercise free choice. The set of needs must nevertheless also be thought to include the exercise of free choice together with the non-natural needs that form its object, and the need for self-respect and self-identity, which for Hegel are gained through work, as is evident from his account of the corporation. In the case of the poor, these needs are, however, far from being satisfied.

The distinction that Hegel sometimes makes between the person and the human being thus allows us to think of the abstract freedom of the person as consisting in such rights as the right to be protected from acts of violence against one's own person, the right to own property and have it protected, the right to be treated equally before the law, and the right in principle to be able to enter a trade or occupation of one's own choosing, provided that one possesses the necessary skills and qualifications. Yet even when a person is granted these rights, this is not by itself enough to satisfy a person in his entire particularity; for each person is at the same time a being with various other needs. Given the fact that, for Hegel, the various determinations of right derive their legitimacy from their status as objectifications of the concept of the will contained in each and every subjective will, of which the particularity of the will forms an essential moment, those individuals who enjoy these rights but do not experience the satisfaction of their particularity will have good grounds for questioning the legitimacy of the existing social order, which, through its own operations, denies them this satisfaction.[11]

It therefore seems that all Hegel could say against the idea that these individuals have a right of rebellion is that the act of rebellion would deprive them of the rights that derive from their status as persons, since it would undermine the authority of that which guarantees them these rights. In other words, he would have to resort to Kant's argument that the act of rebellion would deprive people of the possibility of having rights at all. Hegel recognizes, however, that this argument is a double-edged one: for he points out that the condition of poverty leaves men with the many-sided needs of civil society, while the latter at the same time even deprives them of the natural means of acquiring that which would satisfy their most basic needs, because everything is already the property of someone else, so that one can no longer freely fish, hunt or pick fruit and so on (VRP 4 605). In other words, the sphere of modern ethical life in which the notion of equality is realized not only gives rise to certain non-natural needs, which in the case of the poor cannot then be satisfied, but also deprives some people of the means of satisfying their most basic needs through its recognition and enforcement of property rights. It is therefore conceivable that the poor would be better off in the state of nature than in a condition of right; and this is the place at which one might invoke Hegel's account of the right of necessity, as Henrich does.

Although Hegel's account of the source of the state's legitimacy, when taken together with his recognition of the problem of poverty, points to a tension within his theory of the modern ethical life, his willingness to engage with the problem of poverty allows him to develop the basis of a theory which could be used for bringing into question the legitimacy of societies in which poverty is accepted as being a structural feature of the modern state that must simply be tolerated, as opposed to every possible effort being made to abolish it. Hegel himself states that the question as to how poverty can be remedied is one that agitates and torments modern societies (PR §244Z). In this respect, he perhaps underestimated the extent to which modern societies can remain indifferent to the existence of this problem. Hegel might, however, have reformulated this statement as follows: the question as to how poverty can be remedied is one that *ought* to agitate and torment modern societies. Such a demand is certainly compatible with his conception of right as the concrete expression and existence of human freedom and the way in which he identifies this conception of right as the source of the modern state's legitimacy. As I have argued above, in making this demand Hegel would simply be acknowledging the fact that his philosophy of right has more radical implications than Kant's theory of right, since the demand in question is one that can still be made even when the state has already assumed the form of a Kantian *Rechtstaat.*

Hegel thus appears to recognize how precarious the unity of the subjective will and the universal will can be in modern ethical life; for although civil society has the function of accommodating the will in its particularity within modern ethical life, thereby giving individuals a good reason for identifying themselves more closely with the state, it fails to perform this function in individual cases. This shows, however, that far from neglecting subjectivity, or wanting to abolish or suppress it, Hegel is willing to let it compromise the unity of the subjective will and the universal will which is constitutive of ethical life because he views subjectivity as an essential feature of the modern world with which philosophy must seek to come to terms. Although the tension between the conditions of the modern state's legitimacy and social reality (i.e. the existence of poverty and social alienation in the modern capitalist nation state) found in Hegel's philosophy of right invites the question as to whether philosophy is really able to come to terms with subjectivity by integrating it into a wider social whole, the fact that this attempt to situate subjectivity generates such tension means that Hegel was able to anticipate issues which have become prominent in the modern world. For example, the question of the extent to which the state is responsible for the welfare of its citizens and the question as to whether social justice is possible within a society driven by a market economy. Hegel succeeds, moreover, both in making the tension between the conditions of the state's legitimacy and social reality into an object of philosophical reflection and in identifying the reason why this tension has become so problematic for modernity.

The reason in question concerns the emergence of subjectivity, together with the way in which the latter has increasingly asserted itself in the course of history, and the consequent need to satisfy the demands to which it gives rise.

Notes

Introduction

1 Kierkegaard, *The Sickness unto Death*, 43f.
2 It has been suggested, however, that 'the system' is Kierkegaard's code name for the Danish Hegelian Hans Lassen Martensen (1808–1884). See Stewart, *Kierkegaard's Relations to Hegel Reconsidered*, 457ff. Although Kierkegaard may have had in mind one of Hegel's Danish followers rather than Hegel himself, the criticism that Hegel neglects individuality is one that has been made by others. For example, Hegel's erstwhile follower, Bruno Bauer, came to think that Hegel achieved systematic unity only by submerging all particulars under abstract thought determinations, with the result that individuality is discounted in favour of conformity. Cf. Moggach, *The Philosophy and Politics of Bruno Bauer*, 181f.
3 This characterization of individuality in the strong sense of the term is given in Hardimon, *Hegel's Social Philosophy*, 146ff.
4 Cf. Taylor, *Hegel*, 570.
5 Cf. Taylor, *Hegel*, 570.
6 The German term *Recht* has a wider meaning as compared to the way in which the English word 'right' is conventionally used to refer to a subjective claim in some sense distinguishable from our legal obligations or duties; for *Recht*, like *ius* in Latin and *droit* in French, can also refer to law or the objective conditions to which our subjective will must conform. Moreover, in the case of law, right can be understood as referring to the whole basis and system of law, rather than to specific legal statutes or positive law. Cf. Franco, *Hegel's Philosophy of Freedom*, 173.
7 Cf. Riedel, *Between Tradition and Revolution*, 57ff.
8 Franco, *Hegel's Philosophy of Freedom*, 185.
9 Hegel is here referring to the ethics of conviction (*Überzeugungsethik*) of his contemporary, Jakob Friedrich Fries (1773–1843). Cf. Wood, *Hegel's Ethical Thought*, 178ff.

Chapter 1

1 Hegel almost certainly here has in mind Rousseau, who claims, against Hobbes, that man in the state of nature is naturally good, with this state being the most appropriate for peace and best-suited to the human race. Cf. Rousseau, *Discours sur l'origine et les fondemens de l'inégalité parmi les hommes*, in *Œuvres complètes*, vol. III, 153ff/*Discourse on the Origin of Inequality*, in *Basic Political Writings*, 53ff. Rousseau himself declares that his investigations concerning man in the state of nature should not be taken as historical truths, but only as 'hypothetical and conditional reasonings [*raisonnemens hypothétiques et conditionnels*]'. Cf. *Discours sur l'origine et les fondemens de l'inégalité parmi les hommes*, 132f/*Discourse on the Origin of Inequality*, 39.

2 Cf. Siep, 'Der Kampf um Anerkennung'.

3 Cf. Siep, 'Der Kampf um Anerkennung', 192ff.

4 Cf. Siep, 'Der Kampf um Anerkennung', 200.

5 The *Phenomenology of Spirit* usually forms the basis for interpretations of the struggle of recognition and the master-slave relationship, which I shall also discuss. For an overview of some of the different interpretations of the struggle of recognition that have been offered on the basis of this work see Stern, *Hegel and the Phenomenology of Spirit*, 75ff.

6 Cf. Siep, *Anerkennung als Prinzip der praktischen Philosophie*, 28.

7 This claim is problematic, however. For the fact that another being refrains from acting in a way that would completely limit my capacity to act freely could equally be understood as a sign of disinterest, cunning or a complete absence of anything in common with me, just as animals or trees, for example, do not necessarily completely limit my freedom. Cf. Siep, *Praktische Philosophie im Deutschen Idealismus*, 48.

8 Cf. Siep, *Praktische Philosophie im Deutschen Idealismus*, 159f. For a detailed attempt to relate Siep's understanding of Hegel's Jena concept of freedom to the *Encyclopaedia* account of recognition see Williams, *Hegel's Ethics of Recognition*, 80ff. Although Williams claims that there is no tension between the self-overcoming and release aspects of this concept of freedom, he does not employ Fichte's account of the relation of right in order to explain why they can be seen as compatible with each other; he does, however, elsewhere discuss Fichte's influence on Hegel's theory of recognition. Cf. Williams, *Recognition*.

9 Frederick Neuhouser identifies a number of different ways in which the modern family contributes to the process of *Bildung* through

which people are turned from natural beings into free ones, among which he includes the essential formative role that the family plays in enabling individuals to achieve what he calls 'freedom of persons', which involves forming the particular identities of its younger members and getting them to take pleasure in their own distinctive, contingent natures. Cf. Neuhouser, *Foundations of Hegel's Social Theory*, 150ff. This role thus constitutes an essential difference between the modern and the primitive family, since the latter clearly does not for Hegel perform the role of developing a child's sense of its own unique individuality.

10 Cf. Siep, *Praktische Philosophie im Deutschen Idealismus*, 174. See also Siep, 'Der Kampf um Anerkennung'.

11 Hegel therefore speaks of the drive to show itself as a free self and to be present as such to the other (EG §430).

12 This is another important difference between the *Encyclopaedia* account of the struggle for recognition and some of the earlier Jena versions of it. Cf. Siep, 'Der Kampf um Anerkennung'.

13 Cf. Wood, *Hegel's Ethical Thought*, 93.

Chapter 2

1 Translation modified.

2 In this respect, Hegel's view of the Sophists accords with Plato's view of them as found, for example, in his portrayal of the character Callicles in the *Gorgias*. For Callicles, conventional notions of what is morally right are constructed and propagated by the weak, who form the majority of mankind, so as to protect themselves against those who are stronger than they are. Cf. Plato, *Gorgias*, 483b.

3 Translation modified.

4 Aristotle, *Ethica Nicomachea*, 1110–1111a.

5 Although Oedipus appears to accept that he is guilty of the crimes of parricide and incest in the play *Oedipus the King*, in which the fact that he has murdered his father and married his mother comes to light, this is not the case in the later play *Oedipus at Colonus*, in which he pleads his innocence of these crimes. See Sophocles, *Oedipus at Colonus*, in *Three Theban Plays*, ll. 289ff. Hegel would perhaps argue that this change in attitude reflects the way in which subjectivity was beginning to assert in the *polis*, so that someone as perceptive as Sophocles could not have failed to register this phenomenon in his later works.

6 Cf. Allison, *Kant's Theory of Freedom*, 132.

7 See, for example, Korsgaard, *Creating the Kingdom of Ends*, 77ff. and Sedgwick, 'On the Relation of Pure Reason to Content'. Korsgaard claims to offer an account of the categorical imperative which specifically meets the 'Hegelian objections', while Sedgwick argues that Hegel is insensitive to the different levels of analysis which are to be found in Kant's theory of how the categorical imperative is to be applied in particular cases.

8 Cf. Beck, *A Commentary on Kant's Critique of Practical Reason*, 179.

9 Cf. Beck, *A Commentary on Kant's Critique of Practical Reason*, 200.

10 Cf. Behler, 'Friedrich Schlegel und Hegel', 217ff. and 230. The view that Romantic irony is immoral is undoubtedly in large part due to Schlegel's novel *Lucinde*, which challenges contemporary social conventions. One of its main characters claims, in fact, to have completely forgotten the rules of morality (*Sittlichkeit*). Cf. Schlegel, *Lucinde*, in *Kritische Friedrich-Schlegel-Ausgabe*, vol. V: *Dichtungen*, 8. Hegel himself refers to *Lucinde* in his philosophy of right in connection with the views expressed in this novel concerning the dispensability of the marriage ceremony (PR §164Z). Behler argues, however, that Schlegel's conception of marriage is not as immoral as Hegel makes it out to be.

Hegel's reading of *Lucinde* is also evident from the section on conscience in the *Phenomenology of Spirit* where he speaks of the 'divine worship of a *community*', the spirit and substance of whose association is 'the mutual assurance of their conscientiousness, good intentions, the rejoicing over this mutual purity, and the refreshing of themselves in the glory of knowing and uttering, of cherishing and fostering, such an excellent state of affairs' (PhG 481/656). For this passage is suggestive of the following passage from *Lucinde*: 'They also all burned with a noble love; many great powers slumbered here undeveloped, and not seldom they said lofty things in rough but apt words about the miracle of art, the value of life, the essence of virtue and independence. But especially about the divinity of male friendship.' Schlegel, *Lucinde*, 45.

11 Schelling, *System des transzendentalen Idealismus*, 35/*System of Transcendental Idealism*, 26.

12 Schelling, *System des transzendentalen Idealismus*, 43/*System of Transcendental Idealism*, 32.

13 Schlegel, *Lyceum-Fragment* No. 42, in *Kritische Friedrich-Schlegel-Ausgabe*, vol. II: *Charakteristiken und Kritiken* I (1796–1801), 152.

14 For a more detailed account of the way in which Kierkegaard's discussion of irony in *The Concept of Irony* is shaped by Hegel's views

on this topic, together with a convincing refutation of the idea that Kierkegaard's Hegelianism in this work is itself ironic, see Stewart, *Kierkegaard's Relations to Hegel Reconsidered*, 132ff.

15 Kierkegaard, *The Concept of Irony*, 275. Kierkegaard also thinks that Romantic irony has ethical implications because it becomes important for the ironist to suspend morality and ethics. Cf. *The Concept of Irony*, 283. Kierkegaard's views concerning the immorality of Romantic irony are undoubtedly also due to Schlegel's novel *Lucinde*. Kierkegaard in fact concentrates exclusively on this work in his account of Schlegel in *The Concept of Irony*.

16 Kierkegaard, *Either/Or* I, 292.

17 Kierkegaard, *Either/Or* I, 293.

18 Kierkegaard, *The Concept of Irony*, 284.

19 Romantic irony, as described by Hegel and Kierkegaard, along with the conception of freedom on which it is based, might also be said to find expression today in the standpoint of a post-modernist such as Jacques Derrida, who, while being suspicious of the supposed unity of the self, nevertheless appears to celebrate the freedom and the power of the self. Charles Taylor, for example, describes the practice of deconstruction, for which Derrida is famous, in terms that strongly resemble Hegel's characterization of Romantic irony when he states that 'what in fact comes to be celebrated is the deconstructing power itself, the prodigious power of subjectivity to undo all the potential allegiances which might bind it; pure untrammelled freedom'. Cf. Taylor, *Sources of the Self*, 489.

Chapter 3

1 Kierkegaard, *The Sickness unto Death*, 32.

2 Hegel's use of the term *Polizei* thus designates an institution which is concerned with more than law enforcement. He states, in fact, that the term *Polizei* should be understood as referring to the administration (*Verwaltungsbehörden*) in general (VRP 2 190).

3 Cf. Horstmann, 'Über die Rolle der bürgerlichen Gesellschaft in Hegels politischer Philosophie', 239.

4 Cf. Marcuse, *Reason and Revolution*, 174.

5 Cf. Schmidt, 'A *Paideia* for the *Bürger als Bourgeois*', 478.

6 Cf. Rousseau, *Du Contract Social; ou, Principes du Droit Politique*, in *Œuvres complètes*, vol. III, 371/*On the Social Contract*, in *Basic Political Writings*, 155f.

7 Cf. Hobbes, *Leviathan*, Part I Chapter 14.

8 Translation modified.

9 This is again reminiscent of Hobbes, especially his claim that 'covenants, without the sword, are but words, and of no strength to secure a man at all'. Hobbes, *Leviathan*, Part II Chapter 17.

10 It should be pointed out, however, that Fichte himself considers right and morality to be independent of each other, so that right can be held to have another function (e.g. enabling persons to become individuals) than that of realizing moral autonomy. For a good discussion of this issue see Neuhouser, 'Fichte and the Relationship between Right and Morality'.

11 Cf. Rousseau, *Du Contract Social*, 360f/*On the Social Contract*, 148.

12 Cf. Rousseau, *Du Contract Social*, 374/*On the Social Contract*, 158.

13 In his early writings, Fichte also stresses that the contract through which the state is formed involves an act of self-legislation. The type of self-legislation that he has in mind is connected with the idea that an individual freely enters into the contract and has an inalienable right to unilaterally annul it. Cf. Buhr, 'Die Philosophie Johann Gottlieb Fichtes und die Französische Revolution', 23f. In Hegel's view, this would amount to locating the basis of the state in the arbitrary wills of those individuals who choose to enter into the contract through which it is formed, and, as we have seen, this is a criticism that he makes of social contract theory in general.

14 As well as legally enforcing certain moral ends deriving from the status of persons as ends in themselves (e.g. the duty not to murder) even when the good will to obey such duties is lacking, morality and right are not completely independent of each other because right helps to create the conditions for the exercise of a good will by removing factors, such as the fear of dominion, which may encourage individuals to act immorally. For Kant, politics therefore plays an essentially instrumental role in relation to morality. Cf. Riley, *Kant's Political Philosophy*, 15.

15 Translation slightly modified.

16 Historically the full resolution of this contradiction had to wait until the advent of the French Revolution, which for Hegel has world historical significance because of its unlimited extension of the principle of (subjective) freedom and the implications that this had for the judging of all existing and future constitutions. Cf. Ritter, *Hegel and the French Revolution*, 52ff.

17 For an account of the duties that arise in this way see Peperzak, 'Hegels Pflichten- und Tugendlehre', 116f.

18 Cf. Peperzak, 'Hegels Pflichten- und Tugendlehre', 106f.

19 Translation modified.

20 Cf. Sophocles, *Antigone*, in *The Three Theban Plays*, ll. 498ff.

21 Cf. Sophocles, *Antigone*, ll. 746ff. There is a tendency to identify one party to the conflict between the divine law and the human law as being alone in the right. For a brief account of this tendency and its limitations see Stern, *Hegel and the Phenomenology of Spirit*, 139ff. In his lectures on the philosophy of art, Hegel states that Antigone 'has therefore a worthy reason for acting, and Creon's command is likewise justified, in so far as the brother came as an enemy of his native land and sought to destroy it'. (VPK 95)

22 Translation modified.

23 My interpretation raises a problem, however, concerning the extent to which Hegel's account of ancient Greek ethical life can be viewed as an interpretation of Sophocles' play, since Polyneices does not die defending Thebes or attacking another city on its behalf, but instead dies attacking it, so that the reciprocal relation between the divine law and the human law does not seem to apply in this particular case. There is, however, no reason for thinking that Hegel was seeking to provide an interpretation of the play as opposed to using it as the basis for his account of the essential nature of the ethical life of ancient Greece.

24 In connection with this point it should be borne in mind that, for Hegel, contingency is itself necessary. Cf. Henrich, *Hegel im Kontext*, 157ff. and Taylor, *Hegel*, 266.

Chapter 4

1 Yet this is precisely the type of position attributed to Hegel by his liberal critics. Ernst Tugendhat, for example, makes the following claim: 'Hegel's philosophy is consciously and explicitly the philosophy of the justification of the existing order, quite irrespective of how this existing order may be constituted'. Cf. Tugendhat, *Self-Consciousness and Self-Determination*, 317.

2 Hegel in fact originally developed the idea of an external authority as found in his account of the objective will in his early critical writings on religion, in which he treats the Christian religion as the epitome of an object which, in its mere givenness, confronts the individual as something alien that nevertheless dominates him. Cf. Lukács, *The Young Hegel*, 18ff.

3 Hegel can be seen to hold the view that individuals can experience three distinct types of alienation in relation to their social world: objective alienation, which consists in their social world being alien to individuals; subjective alienation, which comes about either when individuals grasp that their social world is alien to them or when they fail to grasp that it is not alien to them; and complete alienation, which involves being both subjectively and objectively alienated from one's social world. Cf. Hardimon, *Hegel's Social Philosophy*, 119ff. Hegel's theory of ethical life allows for the possibility of objective alienation because individuals can experience their social world as alien in the sense that it confronts them as something merely given and thus alien to their own wills. Subjective alienation is possible because one may fail to gain insight into the rationality of one's social world even though one could in principle do so, or because one recognizes that one's social world is not susceptible to such insight, as is the case with the feudal and the patriarchal state. Finally, Hegel's view of Socrates provides us with an example of complete alienation because it suggests that he experiences his social world as being alien to himself precisely because he grasps that it is by its very nature alien to individuals in so far as they are rational and demand to have insight into what they hold to be good or true.

4 For a more detailed account of the way in which Hegel limits the political participation of many members of the modern state and his reasons for doing so, see Hardimon, *Hegel's Social Philosophy*, 218ff.

5 Cf. Gans, *Naturrecht und Universalrechtsgeschichte*, 93.

6 Cf. Plant, *Hegel: An Introduction*, 230.

7 Isaiah Berlin argues that the equating of what X would choose if he were something he is not, or at least not yet, with what X actually seeks and chooses, lies at the heart of all political theories of self-realization, including Hegel's, and that such a confusion invites a totalitarian standpoint. Cf. Berlin, *Two Concepts of Liberty*, 18. When applied to Hegel, Berlin's argument must be seen to ignore the fact that negative freedom is, for Hegel, guaranteed by the laws and institutions of the modern state of which it forms an integral feature, even though he does not think that it represents a fully adequate conception of human freedom.

8 This 'unintelligible' exception to the dialectical order of presenting his theories is so puzzling that it has led K. H. Ilting to suggest that Hegel is attempting to accommodate himself to the existing social order by giving prominence to the power of the monarch. Cf. Ilting, 'The Structure of Hegel's *Philosophy of Right*', 106.

9 Cf. Williams, *Hegel's Ethics of Recognition*, 93.

10 Cf. Siep, *Praktische Philosophie im Deutschen Idealismus*, 315.

11 Cf. Patten, *Hegel's Idea of Freedom*, 100.

12 The way in which Hegel appears to specify the point at which a reflective attitude entered the world is problematic because evidence of subjective reflection can be found in even earlier periods of the ethical life of ancient Greece, as, for example, in the Heraclitus fragment ἐδιζησάμην ἐμεωυτόν (Fr. 101), which can be translated as 'I searched out myself'. Cf. Kirk, Raven and Schofield, *The Presocratic Philosophers*, 210f. For the fragment in question could be interpreted as not only anticipating the inward turn which thought undergoes with Socrates, but also the idea that in understanding oneself one comes to grasp the *logos* which is the essence all things. Cf. Guthrie, *A History of Greek Philosophy*, volume 1, 418f. In this respect, the fragment would be compatible with Hegel's understanding of Socrates as someone whose inwardness involved the search for truth. Rather than attributing to Hegel the claim that reflective thought first entered the world with the Sophists and Socrates, it is therefore better to say that they helped to make reflective thought into an abiding feature of ancient Greek ethical life, whereas in the case of Heraclitus it remained the property of an isolated individual. Moreover, it might be said that the Sophists and Socrates were able to help make reflective thought into an abiding feature of Greek ethical life only because the latter was in some sense ripe for this development.

13 Cf. Riedel, *Between Tradition and Revolution*, 67. This helps to explain why Hegel claims in his Heidelberg lectures on the philosophy of right, which represent his earliest attempts to develop his *Encyclopaedia* philosophy of objective spirit, that, as regards its becoming, the concept of the free will, which forms the principle and beginning of 'the science of right', falls outside this science, and is therefore accepted as something given (VRP 1 38).

14 Cf. Franco, *Hegel's Philosophy of Freedom*, 185f.

15 We thus appear to have the kind of 'ethical reason' which Robert Pippin describes as having a force that comes from my identifying myself and my good with others and some collective good, so that I come to understand myself as a social being. Cf. Pippin, 'Hegel, Ethical Reasons, Kantian Rejoinders'. Pippin's claim that such ethical reasons are continuous with my natural will, as opposed to being the expression of my real or better self, is, however, clearly at odds with my interpretation of Hegel's theory of right as an attempt to realize the idea of moral autonomy, which consists in a form of

freedom that is held to be radically discontinuous with all natural forms of determination that, in virtue of their mere givenness, lead to heteronomy of the will.

16 There may nevertheless be perfectly reasonable grounds for some people not to act with a sense of genuine commitment, such as the increasing abstraction of labour to which Hegel himself refers, and the bureaucratic nature of modern societies, which, according to Max Weber, turns the modern official into a single cog in a mechanism over which he has no control. Cf. Weber, *From Max Weber*, 228f. Given the fact that the bureaucratic state was a relatively recent development in his own time, it is not surprising that Hegel, who tends to view the bureaucratic nature of the modern state in wholly positive terms, should have been less aware of this problem than Weber was. Moreover, we shall see in the next section that Hegel's theory of right implies that some members of the modern state even have an incentive for rebelling against it.

17 Hegel states, in fact, that the term natural law should be replaced by the term 'philosophical doctrine of right' or 'doctrine of objective spirit' (VRP 1 38).

Chapter 5

1 Cf. Habermas, 'Hegel's Critique of the French Revolution'; Reiss, 'Kant and the Right of Rebellion', 179; and Ritter, *Hegel and the French Revolution.*

2 Cf. Reiss, 'Kant and the Right of Rebellion', 179.

3 Cf. Henrich, 'Einleitung des Herausgebers: Vernunft in Verwirklichung', VRP 2 20.

4 Cf. Tunick, *Hegel's Political Philosophy*, 117 and Franco, *Hegel's Philosophy of Freedom*, 272.

5 Cf. Reiss, 'Kant and the Right of Rebellion', 185ff.

6 Cf. Reiss, 'Kant and the Right of Rebellion', 190.

7 Marx, *Early Writings*, 364.

8 See also Avineri, *Hegel's Theory of the Modern State*, 147ff.; Hardimon, *Hegel's Social Philosophy*, 236ff.; and Wood, *Hegel's Ethical Thought*, 247ff.

Although Hegel assigns to the corporation the function of supporting individuals when they are unable to work, the fact that he makes membership of a corporation depend on the possession of a skill and the pursuit of specific trade or occupation means that he deprives both the unemployed and those individuals involved in unskilled, mechanical forms of labour of the benefits that derive from being the member of a corporation. These same individuals are also denied any form of political representation, which, as we have seen, equally depends on being the member of a corporation, with the result that there is no mediating link between them and the political state. In this respect, it seems that there is little difference between the fate suffered by unskilled labourers and the one suffered by the unemployed in civil society. It has nevertheless been claimed that the corporation represents Hegel's solution to the problem of poverty, since it takes measures to limit the number of goods produced, thus avoiding the problem of overproduction, and to distribute production opportunities more fairly throughout the population, so that this reduction in the number of goods produced does not automatically lead to a corresponding reduction in the number of workers. Cf. Houlgate, *An Introduction to Hegel*, 205. Yet the way in which Hegel limits membership of a corporation and his recognition of the growing abstraction of labour in the modern world make it doubtful whether he himself views the corporation, at least as he describes it, as providing the solution to the problem of poverty.

Hegel does not, however, consider two other possible solutions to the problem of poverty: the Keynsian one of stimulating the economy and creating jobs through the funding of public works projects, which would avoid making the problem of overproduction even worse, and a welfare state based upon an insurance principle. Cf. Plant, *Hegel: An Introduction*, 227f.

9 Aristotle, *Politica*, 1254a. Hegel points out that the term 'nature' can mean either natural being, that is to say, the various ways in which we find ourselves immediately constituted, or the nature of the matter (*Natur der Sache*), which he also calls the concept of the matter (*Begriff der Sache*) and the matter viewed in rational terms (*vernünftigerweise*) (VRP 4 76). The nature of the matter can therefore be held to be completely different from the way in which something is immediately constituted. In the present case, Hegel would accuse Aristotle of failing to distinguish between the condition in which a human being happens to find himself and the concept human being, which states what the human being essentially is, regardless of the differences that distinguish one individual human being from another one.

10 Cf. Habermas, 'Hegel's Critique of the French Revolution', 125.

11 It is worth pointing out that Hegel's critique of the French Revolution turns on the idea that universal equality involves understanding freedom in terms of the first moment of the will alone, that is, the moment of abstract universality. This limited understanding of freedom led to the Terror, which is accordingly described by Hegel as a time of 'intolerance towards everything particular' (PR §5Z).

Bibliography

Allison, Henry E., *Kant's Theory of Freedom* (Cambridge: Cambridge University Press, 1990).

Aristotle, *Ethica Nicomachea,* in *The Works of Aristotle Volume IX,* ed. W. D. Ross (Oxford: Clarendon Press, 1915).

Politica, in *The Works of Aristotle Volume X,* ed. W. D. Ross (Oxford: Clarendon Press, 1921).

Avineri, Shlomo, *Hegel's Theory of the Modern State* (Cambridge: Cambridge University Press, 1972).

Beck, Lewis White, *A Commentary on Kant's Critique of Practical Reason* (Chicago: University of Chicago Press, 1960).

Behler, Ernst, 'Friedrich Schlegel und Hegel', *Hegel-Studien* 2 (1963), 203–50.

Berlin, Isaiah, *Two Concepts of Liberty* (Oxford: Clarendon Press, 1958).

Buhr, Manfred, 'Die Philosophie Johann Gottlieb Fichtes und die Französische Revolution', in *Fichte – die Französische Revolution und das Ideal vom ewigen Frieden,* ed. Manfred Buhr and Domenico Losurdo (Berlin: Akademie, 1991).

Franco, Paul, *Hegel's Philosophy of Freedom* (New Haven: Yale University Press, 1999).

Gans, Eduard, *Naturrecht und Universalrechtsgeschichte,* ed. M. Riedel (Stuttgart: Klett-Cotta, 1981).

Guthrie, W. K. C., *A History of Greek Philosophy, Volume I: The Earlier Presocratics and the Pythagoreans* (Cambridge: Cambridge University Press, 1962).

Habermas, Jürgen, 'Hegel's Critique of the French Revolution', in *Theory and Practice,* trans. John Viertel (Boston: Beacon Press, 1973).

Hardimon, Michael O., *Hegel's Social Philosophy: The Project of Reconciliation* (Cambridge: Cambridge University Press, 1994).

Henrich, Dieter, *Hegel im Kontext* (Frankfurt am Main: Suhrkamp, 1971).

Hobbes, Thomas, *Leviathan,* ed. Michael Oakeshott (Oxford: Basil Blackwell, 1957).

Horstmann, Rolf-Peter, 'Über die Rolle der bürgerlichen Gesellschaft in Hegels politischer Philosophie', *Hegel-Studien* 9 (1974), 209–40.

Houlgate, Stephen, *An Introduction to Hegel: Freedom, Truth and History* (Oxford: Blackwell, 2005).

Ilting, Karl Heinz, 'The Structure of Hegel's *Philosophy of Right*', in *Hegel's Political Philosophy: Problems and Perspectives*, ed. Z. A. Pelczynski (Cambridge: Cambridge University Press, 1971).

Kierkegaard, Søren, *The Sickness unto Death*, trans. Howard V. Hong and Edna H. Hong (Princeton, NJ: Princeton University Press, 1980).

Either/Or, Part I, trans. Howard V. Hong and Edna H. Hong (Princeton, NJ: Princeton University Press, 1987).

The Concept of Irony, with Continual Reference to Socrates, trans. Howard V. Hong and Edna H. Hong (Princeton, NJ: Princeton University Press, 1989).

Kirk, G. S., Raven, J. E. and Schofield, M., *The Presocratic Philosophers* (Cambridge: Cambridge University Press, 1983).

Korsgaard, Christine M., *Creating the Kingdom of Ends* (Cambridge: Cambridge University Press, 1996).

Lukács, Georg, *The Young Hegel*, trans. Rodney Livingstone (London: Merlin Press, 1975).

Marcuse, Herbert, *Reason and Revolution: Hegel and the Rise of Social Theory* (London: Routledge & Kegan Paul, 1955).

Marx, Karl, *Early Writings*, trans. Rodney Livingstone and Gregor Benton (London: Penguin, 1992).

Moggach, Douglas, *The Philosophy and Politics of Bruno Bauer* (Cambridge: Cambridge University Press, 2003).

Neuhouser, Frederick, 'Fichte and the Relationship between Right and Morality', in *Fichte: Historical Context/Contemporary Controversies*, ed. Daniel Breazeale and Tom Rockmore (Atlantic Highlands, NJ: Humanities Press, 1994).

Foundations of Hegel's Social Theory: Actualizing Freedom (Cambridge, MA: Harvard University Press, 2000).

Patten, Alan, *Hegel's Idea of Freedom* (Oxford: Oxford University Press, 1999).

Peperzak, Adriaan, 'Hegels Pflichten- und Tugendlehre', *Hegel-Studien* 17 (1982), 97–117.

Pippin, Robert B., 'Hegel, Ethical Reasons, Kantian Rejoinders', in his *Idealism as Modernism: Hegelian Variations* (Cambridge: Cambridge University Press, 1997).

Plant, Raymond, *Hegel: An Introduction* (Oxford: Basil Blackwell, 1983).

Plato, *Gorgias*, trans. Terence Irwin (Oxford: Clarendon Press, 1979).

Reiss, Hans, 'Kant and the Right of Rebellion', *Journal of the History of Ideas* 17(2) (1956), 179–92.

Riedel, Manfred, *Between Tradition and Revolution: The Hegelian Transformation of Political Philosophy*, trans. Walter Wright (Cambridge: Cambridge University Press, 1984).

Riley, Patrick, *Kant's Political Philosophy* (Totowa, NJ: Rowman and Littlefield, 1983).

Ritter, Joachim, *Hegel and the French Revolution*, trans. Richard Dien Winfield (Cambridge, MA: MIT Press, 1982).

Rousseau, Jean Jacques, *Œuvres complètes*, ed. Bernard Gagnebin and Marcel Raymond (Paris: Gallimard, Bibliothèque de la Pléiade, 1959–).

Basic Political Writings, trans. Donald A. Cress (Indianapolis: Hackett, 1987).

Schelling, F. W. J., *System des transzendentalen Idealismus* (Hamburg: Felix Meiner, 1957).

System of Transcendental Idealism (1800), trans. Peter Heath (Charlottesville: University of Virginia Press, 1978).

Schlegel, Friedrich, *Kritische Friedrich-Schlegel-Ausgabe*, ed. Ernst Behler in collaboration with Jean-Jacques Anstett and Hans Eichner (Munich/Paderborn/Vienna: Ferdinand Schöningh, 1958–).

Schmidt, James, 'A *Paideia* for the *Bürger als Bourgeois*: The Concept of "Civil Society" in Hegel's Political Thought', *History of Political Thought* 2(3) (1981), 469–93.

Sedgwick, Sally, 'On the Relation of Pure Reason to Content: A Reply to Hegel's Critique of Formalism in Kant's Ethics', *Philosophy and Phenomenological Research* 49(1) (1988), 59–80.

Siep, Ludwig, 'Der Kampf um Anerkennung. Zu Hegels Auseinandersetzung mit Hobbes in den Jenaer Schriften', *Hegel-Studien* 9 (1974), 155–207.

Anerkennung als Prinzip der praktischen Philosophie: Untersuchungen zu Hegel's Jenaer Philosophie des Geistes (Freiburg/Munich: Karl Alber, 1979).

Praktische Philosophie im Deutschen Idealismus (Frankfurt am Main: Suhrkamp, 1992).

Sophocles, *The Three Theban Plays*, trans. Robert Fagles (Harmondsworth: Penguin, 1984).

Stern, Robert, *Hegel and the Phenomenology of Spirit* (London: Routledge, 2002).

Stewart, Jon, *Kierkegaard's Relations to Hegel Reconsidered* (Cambridge: Cambridge University Press, 2003).

Taylor, Charles, *Hegel* (Cambridge: Cambridge University Press, 1975).

Sources of the Self: The Making of the Modern Identity (Cambridge: Cambridge University Press, 1989).

Tugendhat, Ernst, *Self-Consciousness and Self-Determination*, trans. Paul Stern (Cambridge, MA: MIT Press, 1986).

Tunick, Mark, *Hegel's Political Philosophy: Interpreting the Practice of Legal Punishment* (Princeton, NJ: Princeton University Press, 1992).

Weber, Max, *From Max Weber: Essays in Sociology*, ed. H. H. Gerth and C. Wright Mills (London: Routledge & Kegan Paul, 1948).
Williams, Robert R., *Recognition: Fichte and Hegel on the Other* (Albany: State University of New York Press, 1992).
Hegel's Ethics of Recognition (Berkeley: University of California Press, 1997).
Wood, Allen W., *Hegel's Ethical Thought* (Cambridge: Cambridge University Press, 1990).

Index